JIHAD

in the Koran

Bernard Payeur

Cover image is of a saber above which, in Arabic, is the Shahadah, the Muslim declaration of faith. Both can be found on the Saudi flag and serve as a reminder that Islam was born in war and that this war will not end until everyone swears the allegiance the sword underscores, or has been put to death.

ISBN 978-1-928023-10-4

© Copyright 2015 Bernard Payeur

All rights reserved. No part of this publication may be reproduced, stored in a retrieval system, or transmitted, in any form or by any means, electronic, mechanical, photocopying, recording, or otherwise, without the written prior permission of the author.

Boreal Books
www.boreal.ca

Dedication

The West is asking its young men, like the SEALs who killed bin Laden and whose helicopter was shot down, to fight and die for a sometimes obscure notion of liberty, freedom and human rights with no guarantee of an interesting sexual afterlife, or any afterlife at all.

The men they are fighting kill and die for the promise of an eternity of orgiastic sex.

This book is dedicated to the former.

Jihad in the Koran is an extract from the Legacy Edition of Pain, Pleasure and Prejudice, a comprehensive review of the Koran.

Other extracts from Pain, Pleasure and Prejudice

Shared Prophets

Women and the Koran

Getting to Know Allah

The Islamic Hereafter

From Merchant to Messenger

War's First Casualty

4:71 O believers, be on your guard; so march in detachments or march altogether.

4:72 Indeed, among you is one who will stay behind, so that if a disaster befalls you, he will say: "Allah has favoured me, since I have not been a martyr with them."

4:73 If, however, a bounty from God comes to you, he will say, as though there was no friendship between you and him: "Would that I had been with them; then I would have won a great victory."

Contents

Revelations and Generalizations 11
   Three Translations, One Interpretation 17

THE ENEMY 19

Vanquished Enemies of Old 21
   The Meccans Who Should Have Emigrated 21
   The Meccans and Allies Who Fought the Messenger 22
   The Arab Hypocrites and Apostates 24
   The Jews of the Hijaz 28
   The Antagonizers 32
   Unbelievers of Yore 35

The Unsubmitted 37
   The Jews 37
   The Perverted 38
      Christians 39
      Polytheists 42
   Reformers 43
   The True Unbelievers 44
   Atheists 46

RULES AND REWARDS 47

Killing Unbelievers Haram 49
   Idolaters 49
   Christians and Jews 51

Killing Unbelievers Halal 55

Killing During the Sacred Months 64

Jihad as Penance 69

Stay-at-Home Warriors and Female Jihadists 72

Emigrating in the Cause of Allah 74
   Someone's Gotta Die 76

Calling for Peace 78

The Booty 81
   Sex and the Booty 83
   Greetings and the Booty 84

Conscientious Objectors 86
War, the Life-Giver 89
   Sedition, A New Definition 90
GENESIS 91
The Enemy Within 93
   Kinsmen, Parents and Children 93
   Women Choose Sides 96
Battle of Badr 98
   Sparrows at War 105
   Spoils of Badr 106
Battle of Uhud 109
   Who's to Blame for the Defeat? 112
Medina 116
   The Jews of Medina 116
   Battle of the Ditch 123
   The Massacre of the Banu Qurayzah 126
   An Avoidable Tragedy 132
   The Broken Covenant 133
   A Change of Direction - The Qibla Verses 135
The Treaty of Hudaibiyah 138
Battle of Khaybar 142
Mecca Surrenders 145
   Spend Freely and Spend Wisely 147
Battle of Hunayn 149
EXPANSION 153
Announcing a Universal War 155
Tabuk 161
   The Destruction of the Christian Mosque of Medina 168
   The Three Sincere Believers Who Lied 169
The Religion of Peace in Persia 171
   Who First Destroyed the Birthplace of Zoroaster 172
A Pitch for Martyrs 174
The Saudi Way 181

Wars Never-Ending 183
AFTERWORD 185
War and Fantasies 187
SPECIAL - INDOCTRINATING THE FUTURE 193
Raising a Holy Warrior 195
    A Very Special School 197
    Lessons in Cruelty 199
    Lebensraum 203
    Willing Executioners 204
        Remembering Nicholas Berg 206

Revelations and Generalizations

Revelations and Generalizations is the opening explanatory chapter of *Pain, Pleasure and Prejudice. What is written there about the why, the wherefore and the methodology used in that ground-breaking publication is applicable to Jihad in the Koran.*

THE PEOPLE
114 An-Nâs

*In the Name of Allah,
the Compassionate, the Merciful*

114:1 Say: "I seek refuge with the Lord of the People,

114:2 "The King of the people,

114:3 "The God of the people,

114:5 "From the evil of the slinking whisperer [Satan],

114:6 "Who whispers in the breasts of people,

114:7 "Both jinn and men."

Both jinn and men! That is it, the last verse of the Koran. What a read! What a revelation! What is a jinn? Jinns are spirits that inhabit another dimension. There are good and evil jinns. The caricature of the genie is probably based on this creature of the Koran.

When I decided to read and study the Koran with the intention of writing about it, I was determined to get a Muslim's interpretation, an interpretation that could only be viewed as being favourable to Islam. I also wanted a translation that was easy to read and understand. The translation that seemed to satisfy these requirements was an interpretation by Majid Fakhry, Emeritus Professor of Philosophy at the American University of Beirut, which has the seal of approval of Al-Azhar University of Egypt, a world-renowned center for Islamic study for more than 900 years.

Messrs Garnet Publishing Limited, with reference to your letter dated 5 July, 2000, in respect of your request that this department (Islamic Research) may review your book titled: An Interpretation of the Qur'an, English Translation of the Meanings. A Bilingual Edition translated by Majid Fakhry.

After having reviewed this book as requested we have the pleasure to declare that we have no objection to approve this book and put it in circulation or introduced for republication.

Islamic Research Academy, Al-Azhar University

In the translator's own words "we have tried to express ourselves in a simple, readable English idiom." Publishers Weekly wrote of Fakhry's notable accomplishment: "Succeeds in expressing the meanings of the original Arabic in simple readable English."

My goals in reading the Koran were diverse. At the top of my list was gaining an understanding of what makes this book so special; to understand what makes the religion based on its content so attractive to so many and yes, to satisfy my curiosity about what God sounds like, or more accurately, reads like. I also read the Koran in the hope of dispelling some prejudices and apprehensions that I had developed after reading about Islam from authors, devoted Muslims most of them, who had mostly nothing but praise for Allah and His "perfect religion".

Pain, Pleasure and Prejudice is the culmination of more than ten years of work and study. I believe it is the most honest, forthright, complete review ever attempted by a non-Muslim of Allah's and His anointed Messenger's legacy: the Koran. This appraisal takes Allah and the Prophet Muhammad at their word, as does most of the Muslim world, and so should you. Although I consider myself well versed (no pun intended) in the Koran and the life and times of the Prophet Muhammad, in *Pain, Pleasure and Prejudice* you will not be subjected to drawn-out discussions about Allah's Revelations. I prefer letting Allah and His Messenger speak for themselves, offering only a layman's opinion, or an expert's explanation, where I feel one is warranted.

When Fakhry's crisp translation is not sufficient, it is Moududi I most often turn to. Abul A'la Moududi's (also spelt Maududi) [1903-1979] credentials as a pre-eminent Islamic scholar are impeccable: journalist, theologian, Muslim revivalist, Islamist philosopher, first recipient of the *King Faisal International Award* for his services to Islam and Islamic studies. Of the more than 120 books he wrote, he is most famous for his magnum opus *The Meaning of the Qur'an*.

The Koran is the book upon which the Taliban, the Islamist fundamentalist movement which ruled most of Afghanistan from 1996 until 2001, based their concept of God's government on earth. The Taliban, like all believers, were, and are required to at least attempt to commit to memory the entire Koran. Believers are also expected to accept Allah's Revelations in their totality without question. This has not been my approach in presenting my impressions, the impressions of a former Catholic, now an agnostic, on first reading the Koran.

As an unbeliever, I hope I can safely express my opinions about the Koran and the Prophet Muhammad, although nothing is certain. It is an unfortunate fact of life that authors who choose to write about Islam, the Koran or the life of the Prophet Muhammad must tread carefully lest the believers perceive their writings as an insult to Islam. I hope that I have achieved that fine balance, if such an equilibrium is even possible.

Translations of the Koran are usually called interpretations because believers claim that only the Arabic version of the Koran can convey the true meaning of God's words. If you can't read the Koran in the original, they say, you are bound to misinterpret Allah's words. Do they have a point, or is it just a pre-emptive rationalisation? A pre-emptive excuse for some of the frightening revelations contained within the Muslim Holy Book. Revelations that may leave some unbelievers wondering if it is God's words they are reading or those of His nemesis?

The Koran is written in verses or ayats, therefore it is true that you will not be able to appreciate the rhythm and rhyme that only the original can convey, but any good translation will be able to communicate the meaning of the poet's words and the meaning of the words is what you should be concerned with.

An English translation of the Koran will run to about 77,700 words; the approximate size of a standard 300 page book. A book, Allah reveals, in which you can study "Whatever you choose."

> 68:35 Shall We consider those who submit like those who are criminals?

> 68:36 What is the matter with you; how do you judge?

68:37 Or do you have a Book in which you study?

68:38 Wherein there is whatever you choose.

It is a bold statement for a relatively small book where boundless repetitions use up print space that could, perhaps, be put to better use.

The Koran is made up of 114 chapters or surahs. When referring to chapters of the Koran, I use the Arabic transliteration (converting from one alphabet to another) of chapter, which is surah. Each surah is further divided into verses. I have chosen to remain with the English understanding of what is an ayat.

There are 6,346 verses in the Koran if you include the 112 unnumbered Basmalahs, the formula-invocation "in the name of Allah, the Compassionate, the Merciful" which appears at the beginning of every chapter of the Koran except the first and the ninth.

In *Pain, Pleasure and Prejudice* I refer to verses by the surah number and verse; for example, verse 2:282. Or by surah name and verse: *The Cow, verse* 282. A verse can be just a few words long or more than 200 words such as verse 2:282, the longest verse in the Koran which deals, in part, with the virtue of good bookkeeping practices and why, when it comes to transactions involving money or chattel, a woman on her own cannot be trusted to accurately remember things.

Towards the end of some chapters you will find supplementary material following a squiggly line (~~~). It is additional information which I consider important that could not be conveniently presented in footnotes.

Just a few editorial notes before we get down to business and let God speak for Himself. All quotes from the Koran are from Majid Fakhry's interpretation unless otherwise indicated. Text added by Fakhry within a quoted verse to improve understanding is enclosed within square "[ ]" brackets. Other clarifications by Fakhry, including footnotes, are enclosed in round "( )" brackets. On rare occasions, you will find italicised bracketed comments within a verse. These are the author's.

Any underlining of words in verses for emphasis is my doing not Fakhry's. I hope that Majid will forgive me if I have substituted the more familiar Koran for Qur'an when quoting verses and comments from his "English translation of the Meanings."

At the beginning of twenty surahs, following the invocation *In the Name of Allah the Compassionate, the Merciful*, are letters, or groups of letters of the alphabet e.g. Alif – Lam – Ra. According to some Islamic scholars, these letters are abbreviations or Muqatta'at, of Arabic words, in this instance, the English meaning can be interpreted as "I am Allah, the Most Seeing." Other Islamic scholars, according to Fakhry, believe they are "secret symbols with which the Angel Gabriel opened the revelation or surah in question." I have included these letters or groups of letters in quoted verses where they appear.

Where warranted, verses are accompanied by sayings or descriptions of actions of the Prophet called hadiths (Ahadith is often use to indicate the plural form, but not here). Hadiths, of which there are tens of thousands, are hearsay evidence collected approximately 200 years after the Prophet's passing of what God's Messenger said and did, including the silent approval of actions done in his presence. An authentic (sahih) or good (hasan) hadith i.e. one that can be traced to a witness of what the Prophet said or did, or did not do, via of chain of reliable transmitters, is usually considered a legal precedent if it does not contradict the Koran[1].

Much of what Allah reveals of his Koran is in the form of telling His Messenger what to say in what are responses or appear to be responses to questions or observations from believers and unbelievers listening to the Prophet deliver the latest batch of revelations delivered by Allah's intermediary Messenger, the angel Gabriel. When you encounter the word "say" followed by a colon in a revelation (with no other qualifier such as "they" e.g. "they say" or on a rare occasions "you said") unless otherwise indicated you may assume it to be Allah telling His Messenger what to say. Examples:

> 3:98 Say: "O People of the Book, why do you disbelieve in the Revelations of Allah, when Allah witnesses whatever you do?"
>
> 3:99 Say: "O People of the Book, why do you debar those who have believed from the Path (the religion) of Allah, seeking to make it crooked, while you are witnesses (while

---

[1] Sunni Islam considers the hadiths collected by six men ((al-Bukhari, Imam Muslim, At-Tirmidi, Ibn Majah, Abu Dawood and An-Nisa'i) with the al-Bukhari collection being the largest and considered the most authoritative as the "six canonical collections." Imam Bukhari (d. 870) is said to have gathered over 600,000 hadiths of which 7,275 are considered authentic. The Koran and these "hadith collections" inform every facet of a believer's existence.

you know it is the right religion)? Allah is not unaware of what you do!"

Is it favored or favoured? Majid Fakhry rendered his excellent translation of the Koran into British English e.g. favoured as opposed to favored.

> 17:40 Has your Lord, then, favoured you with sons and taken to Himself females from among the angels? Surely, you are uttering a monstrous thing.

Not only have I not changed Fakhry's translation to conform to American English (that was unthinkable), but I have, in my accompanying narrative, chosen to remain with British English, with an occasional inadvertent foray into Canadian English (yes, there is such a thing). The same for hadiths. In quoting the sayings and recollections of the actions of the Prophet I have chosen to remain with the English of the translators and their often confusing punctuation and grammar.

One final editorial observation: all quoted verses have been carefully reviewed to ensure that Fakhry's interpretation has been faithfully rendered. Many verses such as 44:43-44 must be read together to form a complete sentence or thought; therefore, do not assume a typographical (typo) or grammatical error if a verse does not end with the expected punctuation.

> 44:43 The Tree of Zaqqum (the Tree of Bitterness) will certainly be

> 44:44 The food of the sinner.

Finally, some of the quoted verses from Fakhry's interpretation of the Koran have no closing quotes and it has to do with an often misunderstood rule of English grammar. If the material being quoted is more than one paragraph .i.e. verses, you can get away with only opening quotation marks (") at the beginning of each verse and only supply closing quote (") at the end of the complete multiple paragraph quotation.

Three Translations, One Interpretation

Is it a translation or an interpretation?

Fakhry:

> 14:33 And He has made subservient to you the sun and the moon pursuing their courses, and subjected also the night and the day.

Yusuf Ali's translation closely parallels Fakhry's; the main difference being "subjected to you" instead "subservient to you" and "also" is enclosed in quotes.

> 14:33 And He hath made subject to you the sun and the moon, both diligently pursuing their courses; and the night and the day hath he (also) made subject to you.

In his translation of revelation 14:33, Muhammad Assad uses square brackets to show what he believes Allah means by "subservient".

> 14:33 And has made the sun and the moon, both of them constant upon their courses, subservient [to His laws, so that they be of use] to you; and has made the night and the day subservient [to His laws, so that they be of use] to you.

All three rendering of revelation 14:33 could be considered translations, but perhaps not a fourth by M. M. Pickthall, a Christian convert to Islam who modelled his translation on the old English of the King James Bible.

> 14:33 And maketh (sic) the sun and the moon, constant in their courses, to be of service unto you, and hath made of service unto you the night and the day.

All translations consulted in the extensive research for *Pain, Pleasure and Prejudice* are from pre-eminent Islamic scholars of the Koran.

THE ENEMY

Generations long gone and new generations of sceptics who continue to not see any good in Allah's Revelations and would rather He kept them to Himself are many, and for them, the Compassionate harbours a singular animosity. In no particular order:

1. The Meccans who should have emigrated.
2. The Meccans and their Allies Who Fought the Messenger
3. The Arab Hypocrites
4. The Jewish Hypocrites of the Hijaz.
5. The Antagonizers: those who held discussions of which the Prophet was unaware.
6. Unbelievers of Yore.
7. The Jews.
8. The Christians.
9. Polytheists.
10. Reformers.
11. The True Unbelievers.
12. Those who don't believe in any God.

Vanquished Enemies of Old

They may be long gone, but the Koran remembers them well. Allah is not a god who forgives or forgets. His Koran serves as a useful platform to vent, for the ages, His vitriolic anger at the contemporaries of His last and greatest spokesman who caused His Messenger so much anguish and tribulations by refusing to accept that the middle-aged illiterate tribesman they knew so well had suddenly been visited by an angel and been given God's latest instructions for mankind.

The Meccans Who Should Have Emigrated

> 2:218 Those who believed and those who emigrated and strove for the Cause of Allah are those who may surely hope for Allah's Mercy. Allah is Forgiving, Merciful.

For Allah, the Meccans who, during the war between Mecca and Medina were tempted to convert to Islam but didn't because they did not want to leave Mecca were as despicable as those who fought His Messenger, and deserving of the same fate.

> 4:97 Those whom the angels cause to die while they are unjust to themselves (the reference is to those Meccans who could have accepted the faith and emigrated, but did not) will be asked [by the angels]: "What were you doing?" They will say: "We were oppressed in the land." They (the angels) will add saying: "Was not Allah's Land spacious enough for you to emigrate to some other part?" Those people – their refuge is Hell, and what a wretched destiny!

Allah was not as pitiless towards all who would not actively join the fight for Islam by emigrating.

> 4:98 Except the oppressed men, women and children who have no recourse and cannot find a way out (the reference here is to those Meccans who were weak and could not emigrate).

> 4:99 Those, Allah may pardon them; Allah is All Pardoning, All Forgiving.

The stay-put believers of Mecca's refuge may be Hell, but they still served as a rallying cry. Allah invited the believers to join his Messenger's campaign against Mecca to liberate people who refused to leave the city even if, as revelation 4:97 makes quite clear, nothing was stopping them from doing so.

> 4:75 And why don't you fight for the Cause of God and for the down-trodden, men, women and children, who say: "Lord, bring us out of the city (Mecca) whose inhabitants are unjust and grant us, from you, a protector, and grant us, from You, a supporter."

An invitation to emigrate to the land of the unbelievers so as to further Allah's Cause that is as valid today as it was then.

> 4:100 He who emigrates for the Cause of Allah will find on earth many a place of refuge and abundance; and he who leaves his home as an emigrant to Allah and His Messenger and is then overtaken by death, has already earned his reward from Allah. Allah is All-Forgiving, Merciful.

Is emigrating in the Cause of Allah meant to be a covert operation, i.e. to establish a fifth column in the land of the unbelievers?

> 4:101 And when you journey in the land, you are not at fault if you shorten the prayer for fear that the unbelievers will harm you. The unbelievers are your manifest enemy.

The Meccans and Allies Who Fought the Messenger

Before His movement attracted a critical mass of followers which enabled the believers to considerably improve their living conditions, mainly through pillaging caravans, the Prophet faced difficult questions. One had to be about why the Meccans and their allies were rich, and the believers, who had the God of the Universe on their side, were poor and were persecuted. They may be winners in the here-and-now, explained Allah, but in the Hereafter they will be the losers.

> 11:15 Whoever desires the life of this world and its finery, We will reward them [during it] for their [good] works, and they will not be given less than their due.

11:16 [Yet] those [are the people] who shall have nothing in the Hereafter except the Fire, and what they did [here] will go there to waste, and their works will be in vain.

11:17 Are those then [like these] who have a clear proof (the Qur'an) from their Lord recited by a witness from Him, and preceded by the book of Moses as a guide and mercy? Those believe in it; but those who disbelieve in it from among the parties (the Meccans and neighbouring tribes who opposed the Prophet) – their appointed place is the Fire. So do not be in doubt about it. It is indeed the truth from your Lord; but most people do not believe.

11:18 And who is more perverse than he who invents lies about Allah? Those shall be brought before their Lord and the witnesses (the angels) shall say: "These are the ones who lied about their Lord. May Allah's curse be upon the wrongdoers!"

11:19 Those who bar people from the Path of Allah, and wish it to be crooked; they truly disbelieve in the Hereafter.

11:20 Those will not escape on earth and they have, apart from Allah, no protectors. Their punishment will be doubled; they were unable to hear, nor did they perceive.

11:21 Those are the ones who lost their souls and that which they invented (the associates they assign to Allah) strayed away from them.

11:22 Without doubt, they will be, in the Hereafter, the greatest losers.

11:23 As to those who believe and do the good deeds and turn humbly to their Lord, they shall be the people of Paradise, dwelling therein forever.

They may also be losers in the here-and-now if Allah decides to do to them what He has done to previous generations who were even better off.

19:73 And when Our Revelations are clearly recited to them, the unbelievers will say to the believers: "Which of the two parties is better in position and fairer in company?"

19:74 How many generations before them We have destroyed, who had better furnishings and appearance?

19:75 Say: "Whoever is in error, let the Compassionate prolong his term; so that when they see what they are threatened with, whether it be the punishment or the Hour, they will know who is worse in position and weaker in supporters."

19:76 Allah increases in guidance those who are righty guided; and the good works which last will receive a better reward from Allah and better returns.

If the unbelievers have more than you, consider it a favour from Allah.

42:25 It is He Who accepts the repentance of His servants, pardons the evil deeds and knows what you do.

42:26 And He answers those who believe and do the righteous deeds and increases them of His Bounty; but the unbelievers will suffer a terrible punishment.

42:27 Had Allah expanded provision for His servants, they would have exceeded the bounds of injustice in the land; but He sends down in measure whatever He wishes. He is truly Well-Informed about His servants, All-Seeing.

The Arab Hypocrites and Apostates

Revelations about hypocrites have mostly to do with the Meccans to whom Allah revealed most of His Koran. Allah's Meccan hypocrites come in many varieties and include, often depending on the circumstances, the following:

1. those who mocked Allah's Messenger and/or His Revelations;

2. those who believed then disbelieved i.e. the apostates;

3. those who changed sides during the battle;

4. those who spread lies about Allah and His Messenger e.g. doubters and cynics;

5. the lukewarm believers who grudgingly said the prayers, did not spend enough in the Cause of Allah and were

always coming up with excuses not to join the fight against the unbelievers.

Allah repeatedly makes no distinction between hypocrites and apostates, revelation 63:3.

THE HYPOCRITES

63 Al-Munâfiqûn

*In the Name of Allah,
the Compassionate, the Merciful*

63:1 When the hypocrites come to you, they say: "We bear witness that you are indeed Allah's Messenger." Allah knows that you are indeed His Messenger and Allah bears witness that the hypocrites are liars.

63:2 They take their oaths as a shield and so they bar other people from the Path of Allah. Evil is what they used to do.

63:3 That is because they believed, then disbelieved; and so a seal was set upon their hearts. Therefore, they do not understand at all.

Apostates or hypocrites, it does not matter, kill them; you have no choice and neither do they, the sly Allah having made it impossible for them to rejoin the umma, the community of believers by sealing "their hearts" i.e. their minds so that they can never believe again.

33:60 If the hypocrites, those in whose hearts is a sickness and those who spread lies in the city, do not desist, We will certainly urge you against them and then they will not dwell with you therein as neighbours but for a short time.

33:61 Accursed, wherever they are encountered they will be seized and slaughtered.

33:62 That is Allah's way of dealing with those who have gone before, and you will never find any alteration of Allah's Way.

Kill them, but perhaps not before informing them of the painful punishment Allah looks forward to inflicting on them.

4:137 Those who believe, then disbelieve, then again believe, then disbelieve, then grow in disbelief, Allah shall not forgive them nor guide them to the Right Path.

4:138 Announce to the hypocrites that a very painful punishment is reserved for them.

Don't bother asking forgiveness for the hypocrites, whose hearts Allah has sealed, you will just be wasting your time.

63:6 It is the same for them whether you seek forgiveness for them or you do not seek forgiveness. Allah will not forgive them. Surely, Allah will not guide the sinful people.

A certain amount of what the uniformed may characterize as paranoia may be evident in some revelations about hypocrites.

9:64 The hypocrites fear that a Surah will be revealed informing them of what is in their hearts. Say: "Go on mocking, Allah will surely bring into the open what you fear."

9:65 And should you ask them, they would surely say: "We were only talking idly and playing." Say: "Were you then mocking Allah, His Revelations and His Messenger?"

9:66 Make no excuses; you have disbelieved after believing. If We pardon a group of you, We shall punish another group, because they were wicked sinners.

9:67 The hypocrites, males and females, are all alike. They enjoin evil and forbid what is good and close their fist (they do no spend in Allah's way). They have forgotten Allah (they have been disobedient), and so He has forgotten them (He has deprived them of His Mercy). The hypocrites are the wicked sinners.

9:68 Allah has promised the hypocrites, males and females, and the unbelievers, the Fire of Hell, abiding in it forever. It is sufficient unto them. He has also cursed them, and a lasting punishment awaits them.

9:69 Like those who came before you (the hypocrites); they were mightier than you and had more wealth and children. So they enjoyed their share (of earthly life); then you enjoyed your share as did those before you, and you engaged in idle talk as they did. Those, their works in this world and in the Hereafter are vain; they are the losers.

Hypocrites are good looking, arrogant, speak well and perhaps paranoid, depending on your interpretation of "they think every cry is aimed at them."

> 63:4 If you see them, their bodies please you; and if they speak, you listen to their words, as though they were propped-up wooden logs. They think every cry is aimed at them; they are the enemy, so beware of them. May Allah discomfit them, how they are perverted!

> 63:5 If it is said to them: "Come, that the Messenger of Allah may seek forgiveness for you"; they bend their heads and you see them walking away, waxing proud.

Hypocrites take credit for other's accomplishments, including Allah's.

> 4:141 Those who wait for [misfortune to befall] you. And if a victory is accorded to you from Allah, they will say: "Were we not on your side?"; and if the unbelievers have a share [in victory], they will say: "Did we not subdue you, and thus protect you from the believers?" Allah shall judge between you on the Day of Resurrection; and Allah will not give the unbelievers the upper hand over the believers.

Hypocrites are lazy show-offs.

> 4:142 Surely, the hypocrites seek to deceive Allah, but Allah causes their deceit to backfire. And if they rise to perform the prayer, they rise lazily, trying to show off in public and they remember Allah but little.

Hypocrites keep an open mind.

> 4:143 Vacillating between the two (belief and disbelief), inclining neither to these nor to those (neither to the believers nor to the unbelievers); and whomever Allah leads astray, you will not find him a way out.

Hypocrites are not charitable towards newcomers. When the Meccan believers (the Emigrants) sought refuge in Medina, the so-called hypocrites encouraged people not to give them money so that they would go somewhere else.

> 63:7 It is they who say: "Do not spend any money on those (the Meccan Emigrants) who side with Allah's Messenger until they disperse." To Allah belong the treasuries of the

heavens and the earth, but the hypocrites do not understand.

Hypocrites think they decide who goes and who stays because of their might.

> 63:8 They say: "If we return to the city (Medina), the mightiest will drive out the lowliest therefrom." Might belongs to Allah, His Messenger and the believers, but the hypocrites do not know.

Some Muslims had difficulty accepting that believers who stayed behind in Mecca or lived unmolested in the land of the unbelievers were also hypocrites which Allah had deliberately caused to revert back to disbelief; the reason He gave for their remaining in the land of the unbelievers.

> 4:88 How is it that you are divided into two parties regarding the hypocrites, when Allah turned them back (to disbelief) on account of what they earned (on account of their sins and disbelief)? Do you wish to guide those whom Allah leads astray? He whom Allah leads astray, you will not find a way out for him.

Moududi:

> They had outwardly embraced Islam in Makka and in other parts of Arabia, but instead of migrating to the Domain of Islam they continued to live among their own people who were unbelievers, taking part in all their hostile machinations against Islam and the Muslims. It was not easy for the Muslims to decide how to deal with such people. Some were of the opinion that since they professed Islam, performed Prayers, fasted and recited the Qur'an they could not be treated as unbelievers. Here God pronounces His judgement on this issue (revelation 4:88).

The Jews of the Hijaz

The Hijaz is the so-called Holy Land of Islam. The area comprises most of the western part of modern-day Saudi Arabia and is centered on Mecca and Medina. In Medina lived three Jewish Tribes. When Muhammad sought refuge in the oasis city he was welcomed by the Jews, in part, because of his preaching that the god of the Old Testament was the one and only god. When the Prophet came to

Medina, Muslims were required to prostrate themselves in the direction of Jerusalem during their daily prayers, but that would change as mistrust and animosity developed between the two Semite people. The disagreement first led to the trading of insults.

Narrated Aisha:

> Once the Jews came to the Prophet and said, "Death be upon you." So I cursed them.
>
> The Prophet said, "What is the matter?"
>
> I said, "Have you not heard what they said?"
>
> The Prophet said, "Have you not heard what I replied (to them)? (I said), ('The same is upon you.')"
>
> *Bukhari 42.186*

The reason for this growing hostility of God's Messenger towards the people who, in effect, ensure the survival of the Muslims when they were most vulnerable was the result of the Jews not accepting Muhammad as a legitimate spokesperson of the Almighty. The Jews of Medina tried to impress on the Prophet, to no avail, that according to their system of beliefs, God only communicated His instructions for mankind via the Jewish people.

This explanation did not sit well with Allah's greatest Messenger and Allah, Who cursed the Jews, and promised them the demeaning punishment He reserves for all unbelievers, for not accepting an Arab as a legitimate channel between God and humans.

> 2:89 And when a book (the Qur'an) came to them from Allah confirming that which they had (the Torah), and though they used hitherto to pray for assistance against those who disbelieved; yet when there came to them what they already knew (that Muhammad would be sent as the Messenger of Allah), they disbelieved in it. So may Allah's curse be on the unbelievers.
>
> 2:90 Evil is that for which they sold their souls when they disbelieved in what Allah sent down, out of envy that He should send down from His Bounty (reveal to them) on whomsoever of His servants He pleases. Thus they incurred wrath upon wrath. And there is a demeaning punishment for the unbelievers.

Until this unfortunate misunderstanding, all was well between

Muslims and Jews. In fact, in the following revelations you may detect a note of sadness about the way things turned out.

> 3:69 A party of the people of the Book (the Jews) wish that they would lead you astray; they only lead themselves astray without perceiving it.
>
> 3:70 O people of the Book, why do you disbelieve in Allah's Revelations while you yourselves know that they are true?
>
> 3:71 People of the Book, why do you confound truth with error and knowingly conceal the truth.
>
> 3:72 Some of the people of the Book say: "Believe in what has been revealed to the believers at the beginning of the day, and disbelieve in it at its end; perchance they (the believers) will turn back!"
>
> 3:73 "And do not believe except in him who follows your religion." Say: "True guidance is Allah's Guidance. [Do not believe] that anyone would be given what you have been given, or they will dispute with you before Your Lord." Say: "Bounty is in Allah's Hands; He gives to whom He pleases, and Allah is All-Embracing, All-Knowing.
>
> 3:74 He favours with His Mercy whomever He pleases. Allah's Bounty is unlimited!

The Jews questioning of the Prophet, who was not always comfortable with people asking him pointed questions about what God had revealed, became most insistent. Adding insult to injury, they often phrased their enquiry in a way meant to upset God's Messenger. It may have been more upsetting for the Prophet's Mentor judging from His Response.

> 4:44 Have you not considered those who have received a portion of the Book, procuring error and wanting you to go astray?
>
> 4:45 Allah knows best your enemies; Allah suffices as Protector, Allah suffices as Supporter!
>
> 4:46 Some of the Jews take words out of their context and say: "We have heard, but disobey; and hear as though you hear not." And [they] say "ra'ina" (a word of abuse), twisting their tongues and slandering religion. Had they said: "We have heard and we obey; hear and look at us", it would have been better for them and more upright; but

> Allah has cursed them on account of their disbelief, so they – except for a few – do not believe.
>
> 4:47 O People of the Book, believe in what We have revealed confirming what you already possess, before We obliterate faces, turning them on their backs, or curse them as we have cursed the Sabbath-breakers, and Allah's command was accomplished!

The breakup would prove acrimonious in the extreme with the Jews earning the appellation, which until then God had reserved for the Prophet's Meccan kin and neighbours, of hypocrite.

> 5:61 When they (the Jewish hypocrites) come to you, they say: "We believe", although they come in as unbelievers and leave as unbelievers. Allah knows best what they conceal.
>
> 5:62 And you will see many of them hastening to perpetrate sin and aggression and the devouring of unlawful gain. Evil is what they have been doing!
>
> 5:63 Why do not the rabbis and masters forbid them from uttering sinful things and devouring unlawful gain? Evil indeed is what they used to do!
>
> 5:64 The Jews say: "Allah's Hand is tied" (Allah is not generous in bestowing His Bounties on them); may their own hands be tied and may they be damned for what they say. His Hands are rather outstretched; He grants freely as He pleases. And what has been sent down to you from your Lord will certainly increase many of them in arrogance and unbelief. And We have cast in their midst animosity and hatred till the Day of Resurrection. Whenever they kindle a fire for war, Allah extinguishes it; and they go about spreading mischief, but Allah does not like the mischief makers.

A people whom Allah's Messenger respected when they first met became a people only deserving of punishment; punishment in the Hereafter and a necessary if unusual punishment in the here-and-now which Allah foresaw in imposing the Sabbath on the Jews.

> 16:124 The Sabbath was ordained only for those who differed with respect to it (the Jews). Your Lord shall decide between them on the Day of Resurrection, regarding that wherein they differed.

Moududi:

> Obviously, there was no need to state that the restrictions about the Sabbath applied only to the Jews and had nothing to do with the law of Prophet Abraham, because they themselves knew it. The restrictions were imposed upon the Jews because of their mischiefs and violations of the law.

This breakup would prove disastrous for the Jews of the Hijaz in the war between Mecca and its allies the Confederates and Medina, the stronghold of the Muslims and their allies the Bedouins (more about the aftermath in *Medina - The Massacre of the Banu Qurayzah* and the *Battle of Khaybar*). Thousands of Jews who called the Hijaz home where slaughtered, with the remaining forced out of the area by Caliph Umar, the second successor to the Prophet as leader of the believers.

> **Narrated Ibn Umar:**
>
> Umar bin Al-Khattab expelled all the Jews and Christians from the land of Hijaz. Allah's Apostle after conquering Khaibar, thought of expelling the Jews from the land which, after he conquered it belonged to Allah, Allah's Apostle and the Muslims. But the Jews requested Allah's Apostle to leave them there on the condition that they would do the labor and get half of the fruits (the land would yield).
>
> Allah's Apostle said, "We shall keep you on these terms as long as we wish."
>
> Thus they stayed till the time of Umar's Caliphate when he expelled them to Taima and Ariha.
>
> *Bukhari 53.380*

The Antagonizers

> 58:5 Those who antagonize Allah and His Messenger shall be abased by Allah, as He abased those who preceded them. We have, indeed, sent down very clear Signs; and the unbelievers shall have a demeaning punishment.
>
> 58:6 On the Day when Allah shall raise them all from the dead, then inform them of what they did. Allah has kept count of it, but they have forgotten it. Allah is a witness of everything.

The antagonizers are people who talked behind the Prophet's back; who held secret talks of which God's Messenger was not aware. You would think that Allah would tell His Messenger what had been said that he needed to know, in a timely manner, instead of waiting until Judgement Day; after all, He was party to the secret discussions.

> 58:7 Have you not considered that Allah knows what is in the heavens and on the earth. No three conspire in secret, but He is the fourth of them; nor five but he is the six of them; nor even less than that or more but He is with them wherever they are. Then He shall inform them of what they did on the Day of Resurrection. Allah, indeed, has knowledge of everything.

The Prophet had forbidden the believers to hold secret meetings to make it more difficult for his enemies and the enemies of Allah to plot against them. A sensible precaution!

> 58:8 Have you not considered those who were forbidden to converse secretly, then they return to what they were forbidden from and converse secretly in sin and aggression and the disobedience of the Messenger? Then, when they come to you, they greet you with a greeting that Allah never greeted you with. They say within themselves: "If only Allah were to punish us for what we say!" May Hell suffice them; and what a wretched fate!

In a matter of a few short years Islam would be triumphant everywhere on the Peninsula and the Prophet's position unassailable and his person secure. God's Messenger, who was in his fifties, would die from natural causes a short time after returning from an expedition to convert the kingdoms that bordered Arabia. Why would Allah include a warning in His timeless Koran about people talking behind His Messenger's back when the Prophet's days in the here-and-now were numbered?

> 58:9 O believers, if you converse secretly among yourselves, do not converse in sin, aggression and disobedience of the Messenger; but converse in righteousness and piety, and fear Allah unto Whom you shall be mustered.
>
> 58:10 Conversing in secret is an act of Satan, so as to sadden the believers, but that will not harm them in the least,

except with Allah's Leave. Let the believers put their trust in Allah.

What those who befriend people who have incurred Allah's displeasure, such as the antagonizers, can expect!

> 58:14 Have you not considered those who befriended a people who incurred Allah's Wrath? They are not of you nor of them; and they swear in falsehood knowingly.
>
> 58:15 Allah has prepared for them a terrible punishment. Evil indeed is what they used to do.
>
> 58:16 They took they oaths as a smoke-screen, and so they debarred access to Allah's Path. Theirs, then, is a demeaning punishment.
>
> 58:17 Neither their possessions not their children shall avail them anything against Allah. Those are the Companions of the Fire, dwelling therein forever.
>
> 58:18 On the Day Allah shall resurrect all and they will swear to Him as they swear to you, thinking that they have something to gain. Indeed, they are the liars.
>
> 58:19 Satan has taken a hold of them, and so caused them to forget the mention of Allah. Those are the party of Satan; indeed the party of Satan are the losers.

Another reminder that the antagonizers are weak and Allah is strong:

> 58:20 Those who antagonize Allah and His Messenger are surely among the lowliest.
>
> 58:21 Allah has written: "I shall certainly vanquish, I and My Messengers." Surely Allah is Strong, All-Mighty.

And for God's Sake, don't take them as friends even if they are part of your family, close relatives or clan members, if you don't want Allah to accuse you of being an unbeliever, with all the evil stuff that it entails.

> 58:22 You will not find a people who believe in Allah and the Last Day befriending those who antagonize Allah and His Messenger, even if they are their fathers, their sons, their brothers or their clansmen. Those, Allah has inscribed faith upon their hearts and strengthened them with a spirit

from Himself, and He will admit them into Gardens, beneath which rivers flow, dwelling therein forever. Allah is well-pleased with them and they are well-pleased with him. Those are Allah's Party; surely Allah's Party shall be the prosperous.

Unbelievers of Yore

Then there are the "unbelievers of yore." What does Allah propose to do to the unbelievers of yore, the people who believed in the benevolent, tolerant gods and goddesses of pre-Islamic times, what Muslims refer to as "the time of ignorance", before Allah and His Messenger came along.

> 44:34 Truly, these people (the Quraysh and their ilk who questioned Muhammad's prophetic call) will say:
>
> 44:35 "It is only our first death and we will not be raised from the dead.
>
> 44:36 "Bring then back our fathers if you are truthful."
>
> 44:37 Are they any better than the people of Tubba' (Tubba' refers originally to the kings of southern Arabia, in pre-Islamic times) and those who preceded them? We destroyed them all; for they were criminals.
>
> 44:38 We did not create the heavens and the earth and what is between them in jest.
>
> 44:39 We only created them in truth, but most of them do not know.
>
> 44:40 The Day of Decision is truly their appointed time all together.
>
> 44:41 The Day when no master shall profit a client a whit, and they will not be supported;
>
> 44:42 Except for him upon whom Allah has Mercy. He is indeed the All-Mighty, the Merciful.

The Unsubmitted

The Jews

> 2:211 Ask the Children of Israel how many clear signs did We bring them. He who changes Allah's Grace (turn Allah's clear signs to disbelief) after it has come to him [will find] Allah to be Severe in retribution.

Allah thought He had a covenant with the Jews; which is why He gave them Palestine.

> 5:12 Allah made a covenant with the Children of Israel, and We raised among them twelve chieftains. And Allah said: "I am with you. Surely, if you perform the prayer, give the alms, believe in my Messengers and support them and lend Allah a fair loan (spend in the way ordered by Allah), I will forgive you your sins and admit you into Gardens, beneath which rivers flow. But if any one of you disbelieves afterwards, he certainly strays from the right path.

Disbelieve they obviously did! But Allah forgave a few of them.

> 5:13 And on account of them violating their covenant, We cursed them and caused their hearts to harden; they take the words (the words in the Torah) out of their context and forget part of what they were enjoined, and you do not cease to find them treacherous, except for a few of them. Yet, pardon them and forgive; Allah surely loves those who do good to others.

He will forgive a few more Jews if they repent and mend their ways.

> 2:159 Those (the Jews) who conceal the clear proofs and guidance We sent down, after making them clear to mankind in the Book (the Torah), shall be cursed by Allah and the cursers.

2:160 Except those who repent, mend their ways and reveal [the truth (which they had concealed)]; these I shall pardon. I am the Pardoner, the Merciful.

Pardoning some while, according to His Trustworthy Greatest Messenger, being an accomplice to the eventual genocide of the vast majority. It is only a matter of time, Allah does not break a promise.

Narrated Abdullah bin Umar:

I heard Allah's Apostle saying, "The Jews will fight with you, and you will be given victory over them so that a stone will say, 'O Muslim! There is a Jew behind me; kill him!'"

Bukhari 56.791

The Jews did not start the jihad, that, in the absence of a miracle, may see them exterminated. The irony is that, if it had not been for the Jews of Medina who welcomed and sheltered the budding Prophet when his Meccan kin wanted to kill him for promoting what they considered a hateful intolerant religion, Islam would have been stillborn.

The Perverted

10:31 Say (O Muhammad): "Who provides for you from heaven and earth? Who controls the hearing and sight? Who brings forth the living from the dead and brings forth the dead from the living? And who is in control of all things?" They will surely say: "Allah." Then say: "Will you not fear God?

10:32 "That indeed is Allah, your true Lord. What is there, after truth, except error? How can you then be turned away [from the truth]?"

10:33 Thus, your Lord's Word against those who have sinned has been accomplished, that they shall not believe.

10:34 Say: "Is there among your associates one who originates creation, then brings it back (to life after death)?" Say: "Allah originates creation, then brings it back. How then are you perverted?"

10:35 Say: "Is there any of your associates who guides to the truth?" Say: "Allah guides to the truth. Who is, then, more worthy of being followed, He who guides to the truth or he who does not guide, unless he is guided? What is the matter with you? How do you judge?"

10:36 Most of them follow nothing but conjecture. Surely conjecture avails nothing against the truth. Allah knows well what they do.

Christians

The largest assembly of perverts in the Koran – those "who follow nothing but conjecture" by proclaiming Allah has a son, "an associate" – are the Christians. Associating Allah with other gods, accusing Him of consorting with females or of having a son is a sin of shirk. It is, along with the sin of kufr i.e. not believing in Allah, the worse sin a person can commit and will not be forgiven!

> 4:48 Allah will not forgive associating [other gods] with him, but will forgive anything less than that to whom He pleases. And he who associates other gods with Allah has committed a grave sin.

> 4:49 Have you considered those who regard themselves as pure (*through baptism*)? Rather, only Allah will purify those whom He pleases, and they will not be wronged a whit.

> 4:50 Behold, how they invent falsehood about Allah (*having a son*); and that in itself is a manifest sin!

Honesty is good, but it will not get you into heaven if you continue insulting Allah with your claim that He has a son with whom He shares power.

> 3:75 And among the People of the Book there are those who, if you entrust them with a heap of gold will return it to you; and there are those who, if you entrust them with one dinar, will not return it to you, unless you keep on demanding it. That is because they say: "We have no obligations towards the Gentiles (Al-Ummiyun)"; and they knowingly speak falsehood against Allah.

As revealed in the verses about the birth of Jesus, some of the first words to come out of Jesus' mouth, only a few hours after His birth, are to announce that he is not the Son of God.

> 19:30 He (Jesus) said: "Indeed, I am the servant of Allah, Who gave me the Book and made me a Prophet.

Allah quoting Jesus:

> 5:72 Those who say that Allah is the Messiah, son of Mary, are unbelievers. The Messiah said: "O Children of Israel, worship Allah, my Lord and your Lord. Surely, he who associates other gods with Allah, Allah forbids him access to Paradise and his dwelling is Hell. The evildoers have no supporters!"

Jesus is just another prophet - the Koran contains references to twenty five others who came before the Prophet Muhammad and it is clear that there are many more – whose words were misunderstood or perverted.

> 5:75 The Messiah, son of Mary, was only a Messenger before whom other Messengers had gone; and his mother was a godly woman. They both ate [earthly] food. Look how We make clear Our Revelations to them; then look how they are perverted!
>
> 5:76 Say: "Will you worship, instead of Allah, that which cannot hurt or profit you? Allah is All-Hearing, All-Knowing."

What Allah thinks about those who believe in the Trinity and what will happen to them for spreading this perversion.

> 5:73 Unbelievers too are those who have said that Allah is the third of three. For there is no god except the one God; and if they will not refrain from what they say, those of them who have disbelieved will be severely punished.
>
> 5:74 Will they not repent to Allah and ask His Forgiveness? For Allah is All-Forgiving, Merciful.
>
> ----
>
> 9:30 The Jews say: "Ezra is the son of Allah", and the Christians say: "The Messiah is the son of Allah." That is their statement, by their mouths; they emulate the statement of the unbelievers of yore. May Allah damn them; how they are perverted!

Allah also had a covenant with the Christians which He maintains was also broken and about which, unlike his understanding with the Jews, He won't provide specifics until Judgement Day as to what part of His covenant Christians did not respect.

> 5:14 And with some of those who say: "We are Christians", we made a covenant; but they forgot part of what they were reminded of; so We stirred up enmity and hatred among them till the Day of Resurrection. Allah will let them know what they did.

If the following authenticated saying of the Prophet is any indication, the explanation will be brief and to the point!

> **Narrated Abu Sa'id Al-Khudri:**
>
> The Prophet then said, "Somebody will then announce, 'Let every nation follow what they used to worship.' So the companions of the cross will go with their cross, and the idolaters (will go) with their idols, and the companions of every god (false deities) (will go) with their god, till there remain those who used to worship Allah, both the obedient ones and the mischievous ones, and some of the people of the Scripture. Then Hell will be presented to them as if it were a mirage.
>
> ...
>
> Then it will be said to the Christians, 'What did you use to worship?'
>
> They will reply, 'We used to worship Messiah, the son of Allah.'
>
> It will be said, 'You are liars, for Allah has neither a wife nor a son. What: do you want (now)?'
>
> They will say, 'We want You to provide us with water.'
>
> It will be said to them, 'Drink,' and they will fall down in Hell (instead).
>
> ...
>
> Bukhari 93.532s

Polytheists

Those who will be pardoned!

> 9:112 Those who repent, worship, praise, fast, kneel down, prostrate themselves, enjoin what is good and forbid what is evil and observe the ordinances of Allah – to [such] believers give the good tidings (that they shall be pardoned).

Abandon all hope who believe in more than one god e.g. Hindus. Even those who are supposed to "forbid what is evil" dare not ask the Compassionate to show you mercy.

> 9:113 It is not for the Prophet and those who believe to ask for forgiveness for the polytheists even if they are near relatives, after it becomes clear to [the believers] that they are the people of the Fire.[2]

The believers in more than one god were deliberately led astray because they did not fear the God of the Messengers, the ultimate insult to the ultimate God, to Whom belongs everything and Who decides who lives and who dies.

> 9:115 Allah would not lead any people astray after He has guided them, until He makes clear to them what they should fear. Allah, indeed, has knowledge of everything.

---

[2] **Narrated Al-Musaiyab:**

When Abu Talib was in his death bed, the Prophet went to him while Abu Jahl was sitting beside him. The Prophet said, "O my uncle! Say: None has the right to be worshipped except Allah, an expression I will defend your case with, before Allah."

Abu Jahl and Abdullah bin Umaya said, "O Abu Talib! Will you leave the religion of Abdul Muttalib (the Prophet's grandfather)?"

So they kept on saying this to him so that the last statement he said to them (before he died) was: "I am on the religion of Abdul Muttalib."

Then the Prophet said, "I will keep on asking for Allah's Forgiveness for you unless I am forbidden to do so."

Then the following Verse was revealed:-- "It is not fitting for the Prophet and the believers to ask Allah's Forgiveness for the pagans, even if they were their near relatives, after it has become clear to them that they are the dwellers of the (Hell) Fire."

Bukhari 58.223

9:116 To Allah belongs the dominion of the heavens and the earth; He gives life and causes death and, apart from Allah you have no friend or supporter.

Reformers

Believers who wish to reform their religion face an uphill battle and risk death at the hands of fellow believers for questioning orthodoxy.

2:8 There are some who say: "We believe in Allah and the Last Day;" but they are not real believers.

2:9 They seek to deceive Allah and the believers, but deceive none other than themselves, though they are not aware of that.

2:10 In their hearts is a sickness; so Allah has increased their sickness. A painful punishment awaits them because of their lying.

2:11 And when they are told: "Do not sow mischief in the land", they say: "We are only doing good."

2:12 It is they who make mischief, but they are unaware of that.

In case the meaning of Allah's words is not clear in Fakhry's' interpretation, a translation by Sheikh Muhammad Sarwar of verses 2:11 and 2:12.

2:11 When they are told not to commit corruption in the land, they reply, "We are only reformers."

2:12 They, certainly, are corrupt but do not realize it.

Rashad Khalifa's translation of revealed truth 2:12 is even more adamant that reformers are evildoers.

2:12 In fact, they are evildoers, but they do not perceive.

As is often the case when the Prophet cannot get people to believe and behave the way he would like, Allah reassures His Messenger that it is actually His doing; in this instance that He is deliberately giving the *reformers* "the latitude"(2:15) to make fools of themselves.

2:13 And when they are told: "Believe as the others have believed", they say: "Shall we believe as the fools (the ignorant) have believed?" It is they who are the fools, though they do not know it.

2:14 And when they meet the believers, they say: "We believe", but when they are alone with their devils (their chiefs) they say: "We are with you; we were only mocking."

2:15 Allah mocks them and gives them the latitude to wonder aimlessly in their intransigence (disbelief).

2:16 Those are the people who traded away guidance for error; but their trade made no gains and they have not found the right way.

2:17 They are like one who kindled a fire, but when it lit all around him, Allah took away their light and left them in total darkness unable to see;

2:18 Deaf, dumb, blind; they shall never return (return to the right path).

No, we are not finished with condemning reformers with confusing comparisons.

2:19 Or like those who in the midst of a cloudburst from the sky accompanied by darkness, thunder and lightning put their fingers in the ears to guard against thunderbolts for fear of death. And Allah encompasses (surpasses them in knowledge and power) the disbelievers.

Normal people will not stumble along in the dark if they can avoid it. I don't get Allah's point.

2:20 The lighting almost takes away their sight; when it flashes they walk on, but when it darkens they stand still. If Allah had willed, He would have taken away their hearing and sight. Surely Allah has power over all things.

The True Unbelievers

Allah also does not encourage the believers to make value judgements, or express a preference for the Message conveyed by one of His Messengers over the Message conveyed by another. A believer who makes value judgements pertaining to His Messengers' Message, in Allah's eyes, is not a believer at all. He or she is worse than a regular unbeliever, more or less in the same league as believers who don't remain steadfast in their beliefs or decide to no longer have anything to do with the *Perfect Religion*.

Allah always tries to make the punishment fit the crime and you can be sure that the "demeaning punishment" promised the true unbelievers will be commensurate with their much diminished status in Allah's Eyes

> 4:150 Those who disbelieve in Allah and His Messengers and want to make a distinction between Allah and His Messengers, and say: "We believe in some and disbelieve in the others", wanting to take a middle course in between,

> 4:151 Those are the true unbelievers, and we have prepared for the unbelievers a demeaning punishment.

The difference between a true unbeliever and a believer:

> 4:152 But those who believe in Allah and His Messengers and do not discriminate between any of them those He will grant them their rewards. Allah is All-Forgiving, Merciful!

> 3:84 Say: "We believe in Allah and what has been revealed to us and has been revealed to Abraham, Isma'il, Isaac, Jacob and the Tribes; and in what Moses, Jesus and the Prophets have received from the Lord. We do not discriminate between any of them, and to Him we Submit."[3]

Allah's reluctance to let the believers think for themselves or to look for a deeper understanding in His Revelations, which on the surface radiate so much hatred, means that making the Perfect Religion even more perfect, as if that was even possible, may be impossible.

Revealed truths tend to reflect the values and traditions of those who first received them and the Koran is no different; as Allah reminds us:

> 12:2 We have revealed it as an Arabic Qur'an, that perchance you may understand.

---

[3] **Narrated Abu Huraira**:

The people of the Scripture used to read the Torah in Hebrew and explain it to the Muslims in Arabic. Then Allah's Apostle said, "Do not believe the people of the Scripture, and do not disbelieve them, but say, 'We believe in Allah and whatever has been revealed...' (3.84)

Bukhari 93.632

Atheists

What about those who believe that all this god stuff is nonsense? They are not identified per se in the Koran. This may be because in the Prophet's time there was no such person. Everyone was assumed to believe in one or more gods or goddesses or some form of omnipotent being. Atheists, by definition do not believe that humanity has an all-powerful invisible creator friend running and often ruining lives, as Allah readily admits doing on so many occasions. However, if Allah had deigned to explicitly singled them out as a group to warn future generations about denying His existence, they would certainly have been at the top of His Enemies List; and deservedly so. It is one thing for one god to refute the reality of other gods and goddesses; it is quite another for a wretched human being to repudiate *the God*, an unparalleled, completely self-sufficient, omnipresent, implacable Supremacy.

Allah, in His Koran, may not have explicitly singled out atheists, but His Messenger's son-in-law Ali certainly did; he burnt them, even if his father-in-law disapproved of the method used, not the killing.

Narrated Ikrima:

Some Zanadiqa (atheists) were brought to Ali and he burnt them. The news of this event, reached Ibn 'Abbas who said, "If I had been in his place, I would not have burnt them, as Allah's Apostle forbade it, saying, 'Do not punish anybody with Allah's punishment (fire).' I would have killed them according to the statement of Allah's Apostle, 'Whoever changed his Islamic religion, then kill him.'"

Bukhari 84.57

RULES AND REWARDS

Narrated Abu Huraira:

A man came to Allah's Apostle and said, "Instruct me as to such a deed as equals Jihad (in reward)."

He replied, "I do not find such a deed...

Bukhari 52.44

Killing Unbelievers Haram

Idolaters

If you don't believe in the God of Abraham you are, for all intents and purposes an idolater. The *Verse of the Sword* states that only an immediate conversion followed by a recitation of the mandatory daily prayers and a charitable donation will spare the life of an idolater or save him, or her, from a life in captivity as the slave of a believer. Having said that, there are three overriding conditions where an unrepentant idolater's life is not yours for the taking at your discretion:

1) during the sacred months if they don't pose a threat, real or imagined;

2) if you have a compact i.e. treaty with a group of them;

3) if they seek refuge with you for the purpose of learning about this Allah.

REPENTANCE

9 At- Tawbah

(The surah *Repentance* is mainly about war, a reason for the lack of the ubiquitous formula-invocation "in the name of Allah, the Compassionate, the Merciful".)

9:1 This is an immunity from Allah and His Messenger to those idolaters with whom you made compacts.

9:2 Travel, then, in the land freely for four months, and know that you will never able to thwart Allah, and that Allah shall disgrace the unbelievers.

9:3 This is a proclamation from Allah and His Messenger to mankind on the day of the great pilgrimage (10th of Dhul Hijjah), that Allah is absolved of the idolaters, as is His

Messenger. If you repent, it will be better for you; but if you turn away, know that you shall never thwart Allah. Proclaim to those who disbelieve a grievous punishment.

9:4 Except for those idolaters with whom you made a compact, then they did not fail you in anything and did not lend support to anybody against you. Honour your compact with them until the end of its term. Allah loves the righteous.

9:5 Then, when the Sacred Months (four months during which war was prohibited in pre-Islamic time) are over, kill the idolaters wherever you find them, take them [as captives], besiege them, and lie in wait for them at every point of observation. If they repent afterwards, perform the prayer and pay the alms, then release them. Allah is truly All-Forgiving, Merciful.

An idolater can seek refuge with the believers for the purpose of learning about Allah, and it must be granted. If after learning about Allah the idolater is still not convinced that submitting to His Will is something he wants to do, the believers are expected to return him unharmed to where they cannot immediately harm him i.e. "his place of security".

9:6 And if any one of the idolaters should seek refuge with you, give him refuge, so that he may hear the Word of Allah; then convey him to his place of security. That is because they are a people who do not know.

Compacts with idolaters must be honoured if etiquette has been observed, such as the agreement being signed within the precinct of the Sacred Mosque at Mecca. But, beware that idolaters are liars, revelation 9:8, who will take advantage of any opportunity to overcome you, at which time, you must insist that they do what a believer does, revelation 9:11, that is become Muslims; and, if they break that oath, then more fighting must ensue, revelation 9:12.

9:7 How can the idolaters have a compact with Allah and His Messenger, except for those you made a compact (*a formal treaty*) with at the Sacred Mosque? So long as these honour their obligations to you, honour yours to them. Allah loves the righteous.

9:8 How [can that be]? If they overcome you, they will observe neither kingship nor compact with you. They only give you satisfaction with their mouths, while their hearts refuse, and most of them are sinners.

9:9 They have sold Allah's Revelations for a small price[4], and have barred [others] from His Path. Evil indeed is what they do!

9:10 They observe with the believers neither kingship nor compact. Those are the real transgressors.

9:11 Yet, if they repent, perform the prayer and pay the alms, they will be your brethren in religion. We expound the revelations to a people who know.

9:12 But if they break their oaths after their pledge [is made] and abuse your religion, then fight the leaders of unbelief; for they have no regards for oaths, and that perchance they may desist.

In Allah's revelations about taking it to the unbelievers, the unbelievers are always those who started it.

9:13 Will you not fight a people who broke their oaths and intended to drive the Messenger out, seeing that they attack you first? Do you fear them? Surely, you ought to fear Allah more, if you are real believers.

9:14 Fight them, Allah will punish them at your hands, will disgrace them, give you victory over them, and heal the hearts of a believing people.

9:15 And He will remove the rage from their hearts. Allah shows mercy to whomever He pleases, and Allah is All-Knowing, Wise.

Christians and Jews

For the Jews and Christians and the illusive Sabians it's a little more complicated. If you are a Jew or a Christian and, as unlikely as it

---

[4] The words "sell it for a small price", or variations thereof, appear in a handful of revelations in most translations. Taken literality "sell it for a small price" would imply that a trade in revelations existed while the Koran was being revealed to the Prophet Muhammad, unless you subscribe to Moududi's interpretation that it means "rejecting God's directives".

would seem, you don't believe in the God of Abraham, then you are no better than an idolater and not converting is not an option.

Unbelievers who believe, and only believe in the God of Abraham (the so-called People of the Book) are not to be killed "wherever you find them" if they are submissive, and are willing to humbly pay money in the form of a poll-tax (a tax levied on people rather than on property) so that their lives might be spared[5].

> 9:29 Fight those among the People of the Book who do not believe in Allah and the Last Day, do not forbid what Allah and His Messenger have forbidden and do not profess the true religion, till they pay the poll-tax out of hand and submissively.

Allah quickly reminds the believers, in the verse immediately following 9:29, that while He is willing to spare the lives of Christians and Jews ready-and-able to dutifully pay his life-saving-tax while acknowledging His pre-eminence, they are still a perverted people for saying that Allah has a son after He told them not to.

> 9:30 The Jews say: "Ezra is the son of Allah", and the Christians say: "The Messiah is the son of Allah." That is their statement, by their mouths; they emulate the statement of the unbelievers of yore. May Allah damn them; how they are perverted!

> 9:31 They take their rabbis and monks as lords besides Allah, as well as the Messiah, son of Mary, although they are commanded to worship none but One God. There is no god but He; exalted He is above what they associate with Him.

And why would they do this?

> 9:32 They wish to put out Allah's Light with their mouths, and Allah allows nothing less than perfecting His Light, even if the unbelievers should resent it.

---

[5] God's Messenger first tried to impose the jizya after the battle of Badr. The Jews ridiculed his proposal saying that Allah could not be so poor as to require their money. The jizya became a fact of life for the People of the Book after the defeat of the Jews at the battle of Khaybar.

9:33 It is He Who sent His Messenger with the guidance and the true religion, in order to make it triumph over every religion, even if the polytheist should resent it.

And then, there are times when a bloody beating, some time spent in chains and a ransom is all that is needed. Killing is optional.

47:4 So when you meet the unbelievers, strike their necks[6] till you have bloodied them, then fasten the shackles. Thereupon, release them freely or for a ransom, till the war is over. So be it. Yet had Allah wished, He would have taken vengeance upon them, but he wanted to test you by one another. Those who die in the Cause of Allah, He will not render their works perverse.

47:5 He shall guide them and set their minds aright;

47:6 And shall admit them into Paradise which He has made known to them.

47:7 O believers, if you support Allah, He will support you and steady your footsteps.

47:8 But as to the unbelievers, wretched are they and perverse are their works.

47:9 That is because they despised what Allah has sent down; so He foiled their actions.

I have killed the likes of them before and I will do so again!

47:10 Did they not travel in the land and see what was the fate of those who preceded them? Allah brought utter

---

[6] The more verbose Mohsin Khan translation is unambiguous at to what "strike their necks" is all about, among other things.

47:4 So, when you meet (in fight - Jihad in Allah's Cause) those who disbelieve, smite (their) necks till when you have killed and wounded many of them, then bind a bond firmly (on them, i.e. take them as captives). Thereafter (is the time) either for generosity (i.e. free them without ransom), or ransom (according to what benefits Islam), until the war lays down its burden. Thus [you are ordered by Allah to continue in carrying out Jihad against the disbelievers till they embrace Islam and are saved from the punishment in the Hell-fire or at least come under your protection], but if it had been Allah's Will, He Himself could certainly have punished them (without you). But (He lets you fight) in order to test some of you with others. But those who are killed in the Way of Allah, He will never let their deeds be lost.

destruction on them; and the like of this awaits the unbelievers.

47:11 That is because Allah is the Protector of the believers, but the unbelievers shall have no protector.

Killing Unbelievers Halal

2:153 O you who believe, seek assistance through forbearance and prayer. Allah is with the steadfast.

2:154 And do not says of those who are killed for the Cause of Allah that they are dead. They are alive, but you are unaware [of them].

THE BATTLE ARRAY

61 As-Saff

*In the Name of Allah,
the Compassionate, the Merciful*

61:1 Everything in the heavens and on the earth glorifies Allah. He is the Al-Mighty, the Wise.

61:2 O believers, why do you profess what you do not practice?

61:3 It is very hateful in Allah's Sight that you profess what you do not practice.

61:4 Allah loves those who fight in His Cause arrayed in battle, as though they were a compact structure.

22:38 Allah will defend the believers; Allah surely does not like any thankless traitor.

22:39 Permission is given to those who fight because they are wronged. Surely Allah is Capable of giving them victory.

David Cook defines jihad has "'Warfare with spiritual significance' [and] is the primary and root meaning of the term as it has been defined by classical Muslim jurists and legal scholars... " *The Encyclopedia of Islam* agrees: "In law, according to general doctrine and in historical tradition, the jihad consists of military action with the object of the expansion of Islam and, if need be, of its defence"

According to the author of *Understanding Jihad*, modern-day Islamic jurists have interpreted what is commonly referred to as the "Verse of the Sword", verse 9:5 which is said to supersede all other verses on the subject of war and peace, and verse 9:111 the "Salvific Covenant" (do this for me and I will do this for you, save you, give you Paradise) as announcing a universal war, a jihad against all unbelievers.

> 9:5 Then, when the Sacred Months (these are the four months during which war was prohibited in pre-Islamic times) are over, kill the idolaters wherever you find them, take them [as captives], besiege them, and lie in wait for them at every point of observation. If they repent afterwards, perform the prayer and pay the alms then release them. Allah is truly All-Forgiving, Merciful.
>
> 9:111 Allah has bought from the believers their lives and their wealth in return for Paradise; they fight in the Way of Allah, kill and get killed. That is a true promise from Him in the Torah, the Gospel and the Qur'an; and who fulfills his promise better than Allah? Rejoice then at the bargain you have made with Him; for that is the great triumph.

Allah's demand for an all-out war for the purpose of making believers out of unbelievers and infidels has been re-phrased in more acceptable terms. Today, jihad is presented, not as a fight to rid the world of people who will not submit to the Will of Allah, but as a fight to rid the world of oppressors (and who does not hate oppressors) or to protect a community from those who would oppress it.

Following are the modern conditions under which Muslims may be asked to engage in jihad:

1. To defend your community or nation from aggressors.
2. To liberate people living under oppressive regimes.
3. To remove any government that will not allow the free practice of Islam within its borders.

A respected cleric or a community leader must make the determination that at least one of the above conditions has been met before the bloodletting can begin.

Does Allah agree with the purported majority view, especially the intimidating "To remove any government that will not allow the free practice of Islam within its borders." Allah's clearest, though still ambiguous instructions as to what the believers can do to the unbelievers (if you are a believer that does not subscribe to the more radical interpretation of verse 9:5) are contained in the second surah, *The Cow*.

Allah is a pragmatic, patient god. It was this same pragmatic, patient approach that allowed the Ottoman Turks to conquer the Balkans and almost all of Europe. They freed a grateful peasantry from the onerous yoke of feudalism and were willing to wait for the next generation to adopt Islam, which many did. In Islamic terms, it was a somewhat bloodless conquest.

Allah's sensible, patient nature is evident in a verse where He counsels His followers to pardon "the people of the Book" and continue doing what they do until He figures out what to do with them; "makes known His Will" in revelation 2:109.

> 2:109 Many of the people of the Book (Jews and Christians) wish, out of envy, to turn you back into unbelievers after the Truth has become manifest to them. But pardon and overlook, until Allah makes known His Will. Surely Allah has the power over all things.
>
> 2:110 Perform the prayers and give the alms-tax. Whatever good you do for your own sake, you will find it with Allah (you will be rewarded for it), surely Allah is cognizant of what you do.

In revelation 2:190 Allah appears to be willing to wait for the unbelievers to die from natural causes before getting "the fuel for his fire", and there is no need for the faithful to expedite the delivery of the combustible unless ... *unless the combustible is aggressive*.

> 2:190. And fight for the Cause of Allah those who fight you, but do not be aggressive. Surely Allah does not like the aggressors.

Then it gets a little more complicated. Verse 2:191, the *Salvific Covenant*, expresses many of the same sentiments found in the *Verse of the Sword*. The main differences appear to have to do with killing within the precinct of a mosque and mass killings, my understanding of "slaughter", to quell an insurrection i.e. "sedition".

> 2:191. Kill them wherever you find them and drive them out from wherever they drove you out (from Mecca). Sedition is worse than slaughter. Do not fight them at the Sacred Mosque until they fight you at it. If they fight you there, kill them. Such is the reward of the unbelievers.

Perhaps a line by line reading of verse 2:191, followed by a presentation of the short verses 2:192 and 2:193 which have a direct impact on instructions contained in 2:191 would provide a richer insight into the mind of Allah when he sent down this revelation.

Kill them wherever you find them and drive them out from wherever they drove you out.

Majid Fakhry, in a footnote, explains that this line refers to the Meccans who wanted nothing to do with the Prophet Muhammad's brand of religion which denied the gods of their ancestors, and drove him out of Mecca. This sentence could also easily be interpreted as Allah's command, that once Islam has establish a beachhead anywhere, to try to remove it or limit its expansion is to invite death and destruction. Death and destruction at the hands of the believers who would have no choice in the matter; Allah's instructions are unambiguous: "Kill them wherever you find them and drive them out from wherever they drove you out."

Sedition is worse than slaughter.

The web definition of sedition is "an illegal action inciting resistance to lawful authority and tending to cause the disruption or overthrow of the government." My interpretation of this sentence is that Allah expects those who would plot or participate in actions to overthrow an Islamic government to be slaughtered. Allah is, in effect, telling the believers that He would rather see the inhabitants of a region, city or community seeking to secede be put to death rather than have them abandon Islam[7].

---

[7] The Old Testament recommends more or less the same thing – that everyone be slaughtered, including the livestock:

> Deuteronomy 13:12-16 "If you hear it said about one of your cities the LORD your God is giving you to live in, that wicked men have sprung up among you, led the inhabitants of their city astray, and said, 'Let us go and worship other gods,' which you have not known, you are to inquire, investigate, and interrogate thoroughly. If the report turns out to be true that this detestable thing has happened among you, you must strike down the

Do not fight them at the Sacred Mosque until they fight you at it.

Allah is referring to the Mosque in Mecca, but I suspect it could be any mosque.

If they fight you there kill them.

If they fight you at the Mosque show them no mercy. This additional command I consider superfluous or simply Allah's way of reminding the believers that he means business when it comes to killing the unbelievers, having already commanded them to "Kill them wherever you find them ..." in the first line of this verse.

Such is the reward for the unbelievers.

This is just Allah being Allah when it comes to unbelievers. Death is the usual reward unbelievers can expect for resisting Islam unless ... *unless they desist.*

> 2:192 But if they desist, Allah is truly All-Forgiving, Merciful.

If they accept Islam as their religion you may spare their lives but not the lives of the "evildoers."

> 2:193 Fight them until there is no sedition and the religion becomes that of Allah. But if they desist, there will be no aggression except against the evildoers[8].

If you are a Wahabi Muslim like Bin-Laden, verse 2:193 and verse 9:5, the *Verse of the Sword*, mean that the war against the unbelievers is a never-ending war until Islam is triumphant everywhere "Fight them until there is no sedition and the religion becomes that of Allah." For these believers there is only the *Land of Islam* and the *Land of War*. Forget about the line "if they desist there will be no aggression except against the evildoers" being a sign that Allah puts a limit on killing unbelievers. For Allah, evildoers and unbelievers are synonymous.

---

inhabitants of that city with the sword. Completely destroy everyone in it as well as its livestock with the sword.

[8] You will find other verses where Allah forbids aggression such as the following:
16:90 Allah enjoins justice, charity and the giving to kindred; He forbids indecency, evil and aggression. He admonishes you that you may take heed.

Remember when you encounter such verses that it's non-aggression against believers only. In Allah's Book unbelievers and evildoers are generally synonymous, and against evildoers aggression is not only permitted but encouraged.

> 3:151 We will cast terror into the hearts of the <u>unbelievers</u> on account of their associating with Allah that for which He sent down no authority. Their abode is the Fire and wretched is the dwelling-place of the <u>evildoers</u>!

To paraphrase George W. Bush who said "I am not a nuance type of guy", Allah is not a nuance type of god. You're either with Him or against Him. If you are against Him you have allied yourself with the Devil and are fighting on the Devil's behalf. Fighting with the Devil against Allah, *the Compassionate, the Merciful*; could an unbeliever be more evil?

> 4:76 Those who believe fight for the Cause of Allah, and those who disbelieve fight on behalf of the Devil. Fight then the followers of the Devil. Surely the guile of the Devil is weak.

In the surah *The Spoils*, which is, in many ways even more menacing then *Repentance* (commonly referred to as the *War Surah*), Allah decrees that unbelievers be beheaded (still today the favourite form of execution in countries dominated by the Koran, e.g. Saudi Arabia).

> 8:12 And when your Lord revealed to the angels[9]: "I am with you; so support those who believe. I will cast terror into the hearts of those who disbelieve; so strike upon the necks and strike every fingertip of theirs."[10]
>
> 8:13 That is because they opposed Allah and His Messenger; and he who opposes Allah and His Messenger [will find] Allah's Punishment very severe.
>
> 8:14 This is how it will be; so taste it; the torture of the Fire is awaiting the unbelievers.

In this surah, Allah lets slip that He considers humanity nothing more

---

[9] At the battle of Uhud, Allah revealed that He sent down angels to help the believers (see *Battle of Uhud* for revelations pertaining to the angels participation). However, Moududi writes that "we presume that the angels did not take part in the actual fighting. What we may suggest is that the angels helped the Muslims and as a result their blows became more accurate and effective" in removing heads and fingers.

[10] Shakir's translation leaves no doubt as to what Allah meant, whether it was instructions for His angels or the believers:

> 8:12 When your Lord revealed to the angels: I am with you, therefore make firm those who believe. I will cast terror into the hearts of those who disbelieve. Therefore strike off their heads and strike off every fingertip of them.

than beasts; the worst of which are the unbelievers who can't hear and can't speak. Yes, Allah could have made them hear, for He is All-Powerful; but, the Compassionate did not do this because He knew beforehand that it would not have made a difference, although what Jesus did, for which Allah claimed credit, would tend to prove the opposite; that healing the handicapped does make a difference.

> 8:22 The worst beasts in Allah's Sight are the deaf and dumb who do not understand.
>
> 8:23 If Allah knew any good in them, He would have made them hear; and had He made them hear, they would still have turned away defiantly

How beasts which can't speak express their disbelief is unclear; nonetheless, you should treat them harshly as an example to other deaf and dumb animals.

> 8:55 The worst beasts in the Sight of Allah are those who disbelieve, because they will never believe.
>
> 8:56 Those, who each time you make a covenant with them, break it, and do not fear God.
>
> 8:57 So, if you should come upon them in the war, scatter (punish them severely) them with those behind them, that perchance they may pay heed.

Other translations of verse 8:57 are even more to the point. In a war with the believers, unbelievers may prefer death to surrendering to the tender mercies of those who prostrate themselves before the Compassionate.

Muhammad Assad

> 8:57 If thou find them at war [with you], make of them a fearsome example for those who follow them, so that they might take it to heart.

M.M. Pickthall

> 8:57 If thou comest (sic) on them in the war, deal with them so as to strike fear in those who are behind them, that haply they may remember.

Can unbelievers expect any mercy e.g. be allowed to escape a battle with the believers? Allah's response is unequivocal!

> 8:59 Let not the unbelievers think that they can escape [Us]. They will never be able to escape.

He followed these instructions about showing unbelievers no mercy by some advice on seventh century terror tactics, and how you will be repaid in full for spending your money on war materials.

> 8:60 And make ready for them whatever you can of fighting men and horses, to terrify thereby the enemies of Allah and your enemy, as well as others besides them whom you do not know, but Allah knows well. Everything you spend in the Path of Allah will be repaid in full, and you will never be wronged.

He just won't let up with killing the unbelievers, encouraging first the believers, then their leader, His Messenger, to kill them in the most cruel manner (my understanding of the meaning of "harsh", which is born out in verse 5:33 and other pitiless verses already quoted and verses to come).

> 9:123 O you who believe, fight those of the unbelievers who are near to you and let them see how harsh you can be. Know that Allah is with the righteous.

> 66:9 O Prophet, struggle with the unbelievers and the hypocrites, and deal harshly with them[11]. Their refuge shall be Hell, and what an evil resort!

> ----

> 5:33 Indeed, the punishment of those who fight Allah and His Messenger and go around corrupting the land is to be killed, crucified, have their hands and feet cut off on opposite sides, or to be banished from the land. That is a disgrace for them in this life, and in the life to come theirs will be a terrible punishment.

And then a ray of hope, unbelievers may be spared if they convert just before you are about to put them to death.

> 5:34 Except for those who repent before you overpower them. Know, then, that Allah is All Forgiving, Merciful.

---

[11] Islamic State, is the poster boy for what Allah meant when He decreed to "deal harshly" with "unbelievers" and the "hypocrites" e.g. moderate Muslims.

Skip a verse[12] and Allah reverts to form.

> 5:36 As to the unbelievers, even if they had all there is on earth and the like of it too, to redeem themselves from the punishment of the Day of Resurrection therewith, it will not be accepted from them, and a very painful punishment shall be in store for them.
>
> 5:37 They will then wish to come out of the Fire, but they will never come out, and theirs is an everlasting punishment!

---

[12] 5:35 O believers fear Allah and seek the means to win His Favour. Fight in His Way so that you may prosper.

Killing During the Sacred Months

In pre-Islamic times there was a four months long festival centered on Mecca, a festival referred to as the Sacred Months (not to be confused with the Sacred Months of the Islamic Calendar:[13]). The Sacred Months allowed pilgrims to make their way to Mecca unmolested. During this period, all faiths came together; all wars and all petty quarrels had to stop.

Mecca, before the Prophet made Islam the only acceptable religion on the Peninsula, was not only special to Allah, but also to all the other gods and goddesses in the Arabian pantheon. In fact, anyone from anywhere who made the journey to Mecca could place a figure of his god or goddess on the altar in the Ka'ba, the structure that sheltered (and still does) the stone that Adam grabbed onto when he and Eve were cast out of Paradise.

After the Prophet fled to Medina, the Meccans, having decided that Muhammad is too big a threat to the way of life on the Peninsula march on the city and demand that its citizens surrender the Prophet to them. They refuse. Rather than risk the lives of the innocent, the Meccans, as is their custom, impose what authors refer to as "the blockade of Medina" but which is more like a trade embargo.

Many of Allah's revelations to His Messenger during his stay in Medina, unlike the revelations the Prophet received during his time in Mecca, have a blood-thirsty, pitiless war-like quality about them. It is during his stay in Medina that the Prophet decides that, if his fellow Arabs will not accept him as Allah's mouthpiece and the Koran as the Word of God on his say-so, he will make them see the light by force.

Even with the so-called blockade in place, the Prophet's raiding parties, which is his response to the embargo, leave and enter Medina at will. The Muslim raiders, however, are too few to effectively

---

[13] Dhu'l-Qa'dah (11 - The Month of Rest), Dhu'l-Hijjah (12 - The Month of Pilgrimage), Muharram, (1 - The Sacred Month, beginning of the Islamic New Year) and Rajab (7 - The Month of Respect).

challenge the large Meccan caravans passing between Medina and the Red Sea on their way to and from Syria.

Minor setbacks, like his initial inability to plunder at will the Meccan caravans passing by Medina did not deter the Prophet. Unlike his adversaries, God's Messenger had a clear vision of what he wanted to accomplish, and more importantly, the wherewithal to outwit his opponents at almost every turn combined with a single-minded ruthlessness that knew no bounds including ordering a raid which would lead to the killing of a farmer during the sacred months.

Virgil Gheorghiu, in his admiring biography "Le Prophet Mahomet", from which much of the story told so far finds its inspiration, condones the attack on what was essentially four farmers taking their goods to market. During the attack during a holy month when all fighting is forbidden, one farmer is killed.

Gheorghiu repeats the same canard as apologists for the Prophet's questionable actions such as author and former nun Karen Armstrong that it was out of necessity that God's Messenger ordered a raid during a sacred month, because the believers in Medina were starving to death. Starving, in an oasis city famous for its orchards of dates and other fruit bearing trees, where the inhabitants more than lived up to the Arab reputation for hospitality stretches credibly.

It is possible that the cunning farsighted Muhammad planned for the attack to occur when it did so as to do away, once and for all, with the interdiction against warfare during the Sacred Months. An interdiction which he could foresee would play havoc with his plans to Islamisize (sic) the Peninsula by force.

The attack on the farmers' caravan occurred more than 250 miles south east of Medina. The attackers' instructions were contained in a letter from the Prophet which they were told not to read until they had reached a well some distance west of Medina. A summary on how it went down based on Virgil Gheorghiu's account.

In November 623, having failed to plunder even a single Meccan caravan passing between the Red Sea and Medina, the Prophet changes tactics and decides to attack non-Meccan caravans plying another route. It is all very hush-hush. Even the men who will carry out the raid don't know what their ultimate target is.

Abdallah-ibn-Djach, the leader of an eight men raiding party, is given a letter by God's Messenger which he is told not to read until he arrives at a famous well west of Medina, two days ride by camel. The Prophet's instructions tell the group to head in the opposite direction. Two weeks later, they arrive at their destination on the trade route between Mecca and Ta'if where they wait for a caravan making its way from Ta'if to Mecca. Ta'if is a small city about 46 miles or (74 km) south east of Mecca. At an elevation of 6,165 ft. (1,879 m) on the slopes of the Sarawat Mountains the area is conducive to the production of agricultural products such as grapes, roses and honey.

There is still a day left in the sacred month of Rajab when they spot four men on their way to Mecca with a cargo of raisins, wine and animal skins. If they wait a day until the end of the sacred month to attack, the small caravan will have reached the precinct of Mecca and will be inviolate. What to do? Follow the Prophet's instructions, which they believe to be from God, or respect God's sacred month. They decide to attack, and one of the four people with the caravan is killed. Amr-ben-al Hadra'mi becomes the first person murdered in the cause of Islam.

When they return to Medina, the story of the murder of Hadra'mi during a sacred month has spread far and wide. A scandal has erupted. Believers and unbelievers alike are aghast that anyone would pillage and murder during a sacred month and that this sacrilege would be tolerated. The Prophet's reputation and his quest are at stake.

God's Messenger is surprised by the uproar but is unperturbed. He orders that the puny plunder for which a man was killed (raisins, wine and animal skins) be set aside and not distributed until he has heard from God. A few days later the Angel Gabriel delivers to the Prophet revelations from Allah that are intended to clarify the rules regarding this killing business during a sacred month.

First, Allah establishes, as a general principal, that killing in retaliation for a killing is allowed during a sacred month; and that killing those who would violate things that are sacred to the believers is justified year round.

> 2:194 A sacred month for a sacred month; and retaliation [is allowed] when sacred things [are violated]. Thus, whoever commits aggression against you, retaliate against him in the same way. Fear Allah and know that Allah is with those who fear Him.

Furthermore, don't let this stop you from spending money and fighting in Allah's Cause, lest you cause your own destruction.

> 2:195 Spend [money] for the Cause of Allah and do not cast yourselves with your own hands into destruction (do not stop fighting for the Cause of Allah), and be charitable. Surely Allah loves the charitable.

What about killing during the sacred months where there is no apparent provocation or reason, as in the murder of Amr-ben-al Hadra'mi? In a fine piece of hair splitting, Allah both condemns and condones the murder of Hadra'mi. In doing so He implicitly, if not explicitly, gives the believers a licence to kill anyone, anywhere, at any time if they honestly believe it will advance His Cause, such as killing those who would "debar people from Allah's Way", which could be anyone, even other Muslims.

He does not stop there! He reminds the believers who would rather live in peace, that fighting "is good for you" and that they should kill anyone at any time, even entire communities, if they fear they will leave Islam, the meaning of "Sedition is worse than murder"[14] in revelation 2:217.

> 2:216 You are enjoined to fight, though it is something you dislike. For it may well be that you dislike a thing, although it is good for you; or like something although it is bad for you. Allah knows and you do not.
>
> 2:217 They ask you about the sacred month: "Is there fighting in it?" Say: "Fighting in it is a great sin; but to debar people from Allah's Way and to deny Him and the Sacred Mosque, and to drive its people out of it is a greater sin in Allah's Sight. Sedition is worse than murder." Nor will they cease to fight you until they make you, if they can, renounce your religion. Those of you who renounce their religion and die, while they are unbelievers, are those whose works come to grief, [both] in this world and in the Hereafter. And they are the people of the Fire, abiding in it forever.

The murder of Hadra'mi, and Allah's failure to categorically condemn the killing during a sacred month, meant that jihad could be

---

[14] The Koran is somewhat unique in the way it elevates murder, revealed truth 2:217 "sedition is worse than murder", and mass murder, revealed truth 2:191 "Sedition is worse than slaughter" into a virtue.

conducted throughout the year. This could have been the farsighted Prophet's objective all along.

~~~~~~~~~~~~~~~~~

Ta'if would prove a difficult conquest, even for experienced holy warriors, during the campaign to convert the people of the Arabian Peninsula by force.

Narrated Abdullah bin Umar:

When Allah Apostle was in Ta'if (trying to conquer it), he said to his companions, "Tomorrow we will return (to Medina), if Allah wills."

Some of the companions of Allah's Apostle said, "We will not leave till we conquer it."

The Prophet said, "Therefore, be ready to fight tomorrow."

On the following day, they (Muslims) fought fiercely (with the people of Ta'if) and suffered many wounds.

Then Allah's Apostle said, "Tomorrow we will return (to Medina), if Allah wills."

His companions kept quiet this time. Allah's Apostle then smiled.

Bukhari 73.109

Jihad as Penance

The concept of jihad and the promise of a "great reward" for killing and dying for Allah have fascinated Islamic scholars and writers from the earliest military conquests carried out during the life, and after the Prophet's death, to this day.

> 4:74 So let those who sell the present for the life to come fight in the Way of Allah. Whoever fights in the Way of Allah and is killed or conquers, We shall accord him a great reward.

The earliest known writer on *jihad*, according to Cook, is Abdallah b. al-Mubarak author of the Kitab al-Jihad (Book of Holy War). From his interpretation of Koranic verses such as verse 4:74 and his study of the sayings and examples of the Prophet Muhammad – including a statement about the sword wiping away sins – Mubarak made the following observations about the redemptive value of killing and dying in the name of Allah.

> The slain [in jihad] are three [types of] men. A believer, who struggles with himself and his possessions in the path of God, such that when he meets the enemy [in battle] he fights them until he is killed. This martyr (*shahid*) is tested, [and is] in the camp of God under His throne; the prophets do not exceed him [in merit] except by the level of prophecy. [Then] a believer, committing offences and sins against himself, who struggles with himself and his possessions in the path of God; such that when he meets the enemy [in battle] he fights until he is killed. This cleansing wipes away his offences and his sins – behold the sword wipes [away] sins! – and he will be let into heaven by whatever gate he wishes. ... [Then] a hypocrite who struggles with himself and his possessions in the path of God; such that when he meets the enemy [in battle] he

> fights until he is killed. This [man] is in hell since the sword does not wipe away hypocrisy.
>
> David Cook, cf. Ibn al-Mubarak Understanding Jihad, p.14.

Later writings would expand on this concept that killing and being killed "in the path of Allah" has two redeeming features: atonement for your sins and rank in heaven[15]. In the Christian gospels, Jesus of Nazareth shed his blood to redeem the sins of mankind; in the Islamic variation, it is the shedding of one's own blood while killing the enemies of Allah that wipes away sins (the exception being one who dies in "the path of Allah" but whose loyalty was not always constant – the hypocrite).

> There is a man who fights in the path of Allah and does not want to kill or be killed, but is struck by an arrow. The first drop of blood from him is atonement for every sin he has committed; for every drop he sheds he gains levels in paradise. The second type of man is one who fights desiring to kill but not to be killed, and is struck by an arrow. The first drop of blood from him is for every sin; for every drop he sheds he gains a level in paradise until he bumps Abraham's knee. The third type of man is one who fights in the path of Allah <u>desiring to kill and be killed</u> and is struck by an arrow. The first drop of blood from him is atonement for every sin; he will come to the Day of Resurrection with a drawn sword [able to] intercede.
>
> David Cook, cf. Ibn al-Mubarak Understanding Jihad, p.15.

This belief in the atonement properties of killing and dying for Allah and the way you died having an influence on your ranking in heaven, could, according to the author of *Understanding Jihad*, have been responsible for "inspiring the conquest of so much territory and achieving what the early Muslims achieved."

Killing and the way you die atoning for one's sins is also, in my estimation, responsible for the willingness of men and women to sacrifice themselves in suicide attacks that claim both theirs and the lives of the assumed enemies of Allah. It is doubly effective since it appeals to both the constant, exemplary believer and the born-again believer.

---

[15] Heaven has seven levels. The highest level is where Allah sits on His Throne with His Messenger and Abraham at His side.

The exemplary believer who has led a life according to the dictates of the Koran and the Prophet's Sunnah, by his murderous self-immolation not only offers a last honour and proof of his loyalty to Allah and His Messenger but is also assured of a higher ranking in heaven. The born-again believer, on the other hand, can in one irrational destructive act, atone for an entire life of sinful behaviour including pre-meditated murder[16] and gain immediate, unrestricted access to Paradise. Add to this, the appeal to the sexually obsessed who do it for a promise of unlimited sex with virginal girls and "blushing maidens" in heaven, and it's a wonder that there are not more Muslims willing to take on the role of the grim reaper.

Allah may have wanted the believers to kill and die on his behalf and be handsomely rewarded for doing so, but he does not want them to get themselves killed fighting each other.

> 4:29 O believers, do not consume your wealth illegally, unless there be trading by mutual agreement among you; and do not kill yourselves. Allah is indeed merciful to you!

If only the next verse in this series was also a warning to the believers not to act aggressively against those who don't share their religious obsessions.

> 4:30 And whoever acts aggressively and wrongfully, We shall cast him in the Fire; this being an easy matter for Allah.

---

[16] **Narrated Abu Huraira:**

Allah's Apostle said, "Allah welcomes two men with a smile; one of whom kills the other and both of them enter Paradise. One fights in Allah's Cause and gets killed. Later on Allah forgives the killer who also get martyred (In Allah's Cause)."

Bukhari 52.80

Stay-at-Home Warriors and Female Jihadists

Ibn al-Mubarak came up with a ranking for those who kill and die for Allah. What about your stay-at-home warriors? Perhaps surprisingly, Allah and His Messenger do not damn them to an eternity in Hell. Their rank in heaven, however, will definitely be lower than a believer who kills and risks his life in the fight to extend Allah's domain, and the rewards stay-at-home warriors can expect in heaven are somewhat diminished.

> 4:95 Those of the believers who stay at home while suffering from no injury are not equal to those who fight for the Cause of Allah with their possessions and persons. Allah has raised those who fight with their possessions and persons one degree over those who stay at home; and to each Allah has promised the fairest good. Yet Allah has granted a great reward to those who fight and not to those who stay behind.

As you may have come to expect, verses about killing in the cause of Allah, followed by verses extolling the virtues of an "All-Forgiving, Merciful" god

> 4:96 Degrees of honour from Him, Forgiveness and Mercy. Allah is All-Forgiving, Merciful.

What rewards can a female jihadist expect from Allah for fighting and dying to extend his dominion on earth? Again, according to David Cook, a question was posed on the Hamas website by a prospective female suicide bomber as to what are the "rewards for a female martyr." Would she get the equivalent of the male suicide bombers who are promised a "fairly extensive harem of women in return for martyrdom."

[Question] I wanted to ask: what is the reward of a female martyr who performs a martyrdom operation; does she marry 72 of the houris?

[Answer] ... the female martyr gains the same rewards as does the male, with the exception of this one aspect [the *houris*], so that the female martyr will be with the same husband with whom she dies. "And those who have believed and their progeny, followed them in belief. We shall join their progeny to them. We shall not deprive them of any of their work; every man shall be bound by what he has earned" [52:21]. <u>The one who is martyred and has no husband will be married to one of the people of Paradise.</u>

David Cook, Understanding Jihad, p.146

Unless I am mistaken, that would be the same reward that a stay-at-home housewife could expect from Allah, therefore there is nothing to be gained by a chaste girl or a pious married women blowing herself up and killing herself and a bunch of innocent people for Allah.

Emigrating in the Cause of Allah

8:72 Those who have believed and emigrated and struggled with their wealth and their lives in the Path of Allah, and those who gave refuge and support – those are friends of one another; but those who have believed, yet did not emigrate, you will not be responsible for their protection until they emigrate. Should they seek your support for religion's sake, you ought to support them, but not against a people with whom you have a compact. Allah is Fully Aware of what you do.

8:74 And those who believed, emigrated and struggled in the Path of Allah, and those who have given refuge and support – those are the true believers. They will have forgiveness and bountiful provision.

8:75 And those who believed afterwards, emigrated and struggle with you – those are part of you. And the blood relatives are closer to one another in Allah's Book. Allah is truly Cognizant of everything.

9:20 Those who have believed, emigrated and fought in the Path of Allah with their lives are higher in rank in Allah's Sight; and those are the winners.

9:21 Their Lord announces to them the good news of a mercy from Him, good pleasure and Gardens wherein they have everlasting bliss;

9:22 Abiding therein forever. With Allah is a great reward.

9:100 The early Emigrants (the early Muslims who emigrated to Medina) and the Helpers (the Muslims of Medina who supported the Emigrants) and those who followed them up in beneficence – Allah is well-pleased with them, and they are well-pleased with Him, and He has prepared for them Gardens beneath which rivers flow, abiding therein forever. That is the great triumph!

16:41 To those who emigrated for Allah's Sake, after they had been oppressed, We shall provide a good life in this world; but the reward of the Hereafter is greater, if only they knew.

16:42 [They are] those who are patient, and in their Lord they put their trust.

16:110 As for those who emigrated after they had been persecuted, then fought in the Way of Allah and stood fast, your Lord is Forgiving, Merciful.

16:111 The Day every soul shall come pleading for itself, and every soul shall be paid in full for what it did, they shall not be dealt with unjustly.

The previous revelations were meant to encourage converts to Islam to emigrate out of pagan controlled areas and join the Prophet's forces at Medina and fight to the death, if necessary, for the advancement of Islam, or emigrate into areas controlled by the pagan Arabs as a means of weakening the opposition to the Prophet's takeover of the Peninsula.

Today, these verses are interpreted by Islamists as inviting believers to emigrate where unbelievers are the majority as a means of weakening the opposition in the struggle to bring all of mankind to submit to Allah's Will. This would also be in keeping with the Prophet's instructions:

I charge you with five of what Allah has charged me with; to assemble, to listen, to obey, to immigrate and to wage Jihad for the sake of Allah. *Tirmidi*

Migration will continue until the sun rises from the West. Hijra will not be stopped until repentance is cut off, and repentance will not be cut off until the sun rises from the West (on Judgement Day). *Dawud*

O people, immigrate, holding on to Islam, for Hijra (migration) is to continue as long as Jihad continues. *Malik*

... if you settle then spread out. *Bukhari*

Someone's Gotta Die

In inviting the emigrants to die for Him, Allah brings a new twist to Talion law.

> 22:58 And those who emigrated in the Path of Allah, then were killed or died, Allah shall provide them with a fair provision. Allah is surely the Best Provider.
>
> 22:59 He will admit them into a place with which they will be well-pleased. Surely, Allah is All-Knowing, Clement.
>
> 22:60 All that; and he who chastises in the same way he was chastised, then he is wronged, Allah shall support him. Allah is surely a Pardoner, All-Forgiver.

At least two schools of Sharia law disagree on the exact meaning of revelation 22:60. Both agree that someone's gotta die, it's the how, as Moududi explains:

> ... the reference is to those victims of persecution who could fight back. From this verse, Imam Shafi`i has concluded that "retaliation" will be effected in the way as life was taken in the original act. If a person is killed by immersion in water, the killer also should be put to death by immersion in water; or if a person is burnt to death, the killer also will be burnt to death.
>
> The Hanafites dispute this. According to them, retaliation against a murderer will be incurred in one and the same established way no matter how life was taken by the culprit in the original act.

What does any of this have to do with night and day, revelation 22:61, and other gods, revelation 22:62.

> 22:61 That is because Allah causes the night to pass into the day and the day to pass into the night, and that Allah is All-Hearing, All-Seeing.

22:62 That is because Allah is the Truth and what they call upon besides Him is the falsehood; and that Allah is the Exalted, the Great One.

Probably nothing; Allah's mind may again have wondered off in a different direction, what Justin Wintle author of *History of Islam* defines as "jumping from one subject to another in a sort of unfurling stream of supra-consciousness", or it may be simply that Allah has a short attention span. Whatever the reason for the disconnect, those who are about to die because of something He said deserve better.

Calling for Peace

The Verse of the Sword, the Salvific Covenant and the letter from God's Messenger threatening to impose Islam by force would indicate that Muslims who fight, kill and die in the pursuit of a universal Islam are legally and morally justified in doing so. Until Allah or His Messenger declares an end to the hostilities against the unbelievers they have no choice in the matter.

Writers on Islam, like Fouad Laroui, would disagree with what appears to be the Prophet and Allah's sanctioning of extreme measures to establish His kingdom on earth in many of the verses presented so far. In his book *On Islamic Fundamentalism – A personal denunciation of religious extremism* (my understanding of *De L'Islamisme – Une réfutation personnelle du totalitarisme religieux*) Laroui quotes from verse 4:171 to support his argument that Allah does not approve of violence to get others to accept Islam as their religion.

> 4:171 O People of the Book, do not exceed the bounds of your religion...

So far so good; but like in so many revelations, Allah muddles the message by qualifying his instructions about not exceeding "the bounds of your religion" by adding that you must still tell the truth, your religion's unassailable truth which contradicts another religion's unassailable truth.

> 4:171 ... nor say about Allah except the truth. The Messiah, Jesus, son of Mary, is only Allah's Messenger and His Word, which he imparted to Mary, and is a spirit from Him! So believe in Allah and His Messengers and do not say "three" [gods]. Refrain; it is better for you. Allah is truly One God. How – Glory be to Him – could He have a son To him belongs what is in Heaven and on earth? Allah suffices as a Guardian!

In the never-ending-war to spread Allah's unassailable truth and make Islam "triumph over every religion" should you seek peace with the unbelievers? *Only if you are losing* or they call for peace, revelation 8:61, but be wary, revelation 8:62.

> 47:35 So do not weaken and call for peace, while you have the upper hand and Allah is with you. He will not stint you your actions.
>
> 47:36 Indeed, this present life is but sport and amusement; and if you believe and are God-fearing, He will give you your wages and will not ask you for your possessions.

> 8:61 And if they incline to peace, incline to it too, and put your trust in a Allah. He is truly the Hearer, the Knower.
>
> 8:62 And if they wish to deceive you, then Allah is Sufficient for you and so are the believers, it is He who has strengthened you with His Support and with the believers;
>
> 8:63 He brought their hearts together. Had you spent all there is on earth, you could not have brought their hearts together, but Allah has brought them together. He is Mighty and Wise.

Moududi:

> Here the allusion is to that strong bond of love and brotherhood that developed among the Arabs who embraced Islam and whose conversion brought them solidarity. This strong solidarity existed despite the fact that they came from a variety of tribes which had long-standing traditions of mutual enmity.

Considering the superiority of believers as warriors and the fact that they have the only god that matters on their side meant that the call for peace was and would remain a call seldom made.

> 8:64 O Prophet, Allah is Sufficient for you and so are the believers who follow you.
>
> 8:65 O Prophet, urge the believers to fight. If there are twenty steadfast men among you, they will defeat two hundred; and if there are a hundred, they will defeat a thousand of the unbelievers, because they are a people who do not understand.

8:66 Now Allah has lightened your burden; He knows that there is a weakness in you. So, if there are a hundred steadfast men among you, they will overcome two hundred; and if there are a thousand men among you, they will overcome two thousand, by Allah's Leave. Allah is with the steadfast.

The Booty

Booty, which includes the wives and daughters of the unbelievers you killed or enslaved, played a significant part in attracting men to Islam.

Narrated Marwan bin Al-Hakam and Al-Miswar bin Makhrama:

When the delegates of the tribe of Hawazin after embracing Islam, came to Allah's Apostle, he got up. They appealed to him to return their properties and their captives.

Allah's Apostle said to them, "The most beloved statement to me is the true one. So, you have the option of restoring your properties or your captives, for I have delayed distributing them."

The narrator added, Allah's Apostle had been waiting for them for more than ten days on his return from Taif.

When they realized that Allah's Apostle would return to them only one of two things, they said, "We choose our captives." So, Allah's Apostle got up in the gathering of the Muslims, praised Allah as He deserved, and said, "Then after! These brethren of yours have come to you with repentance and I see it proper to return their captives to them. So, whoever amongst you likes to do that as a favor, then he can do it, and whoever of you wants to stick to his share till we pay him from the very first booty which Allah will give us then he can do so."

The people replied, "We agree to give up our shares willingly as a favor for Allah's Apostle."

Then Allah's Apostle said, "We don't know who amongst you has agreed and who hasn't. Go back and your chiefs may tell us your opinion."

> So, all of them returned and their chiefs discussed the matter with them and then they (i.e. their chiefs) came to Allah's Apostle to tell him that they (i.e. the people) had given up their shares gladly and willingly.

Bukhari 38.503

In making war on the unbelievers, Allah reminded the believers not to let the booty distract them from their immediate goal which is shedding the blood of those who refuse to submit to His Will.

> 8:67 It is not up to any Prophet to take captives except after too much blood is shed (after the enemy is hard hit and subdued) in the land. You desire the fleeting goods of this world, but Allah desires the Hereafter, and Allah is Mighty, Wise.

Revealed truths which confirm the inalienable right of a believer to the property (both eatable and uneatable) and the wife and kids of an unbeliever he has slaughtered.

> 8:68 But for a prior ordinance of Allah, you would have been afflicted on account of what you have taken (an ordinance which made it lawful for Muslims to take spoils and captives) by a terrible punishment.
>
> 8:69 So eat of the lawful and good things you have taken as booty. Fear Allah; Allah is truly All-Forgiving, Merciful[17].

If sharing in the booty is not sufficient to convince you to submit to Allah's Will, remember that in Allah's eyes you are traitors, with all the horrifying stuff that implies, with your continued enslavement the best that you can hope for.

> 8:70 O Prophet, tell those captives in your keeping: "If Allah knows of any good in your hearts, He will give you in

---

[17] The right of the believer to the property of a slain unbeliever is also confirmed in a saying of the Prophet in which he boast that "the keys of the treasures of the world were brought to me and put in my hand."

Narrated Abu Huraira:

Allah's Apostle said, "I have been sent with the shortest expressions bearing the widest meanings, and I have been made victorious with terror (cast in the hearts of the enemy), and while I was sleeping, the keys of the treasures of the world were brought to me and put in my hand."

Bukhari 52.220

return better than what has been taken from you and forgive you." Allah is All-Forgiving, Merciful.

8:71 But if they wish to betray you, they have previously betrayed Allah, and so He subdued them. Allah is All-Knowing, Wise.

Sex and the Booty

It was a given that you could have sex with your female booty, with or without the booty's consent. However, until God's Messenger offered his considered opinion some holy warriors were unsure about whether coitus interruptus was halal. They consulted with the Prophet who made his, and what has to be assumed is God's view clear on a believer withdrawing his member from his captive's vagina prior to ejaculation.

Narrated Abu Said Al-Khudri:

that while he was sitting with Allah's Apostle he said, "O Allah's Apostle! We get female captives as our share of booty, and we are interested in their prices, what is your opinion about coitus interruptus?"

The Prophet said, "Do you really do that? It is better for you not to do it. No soul that which Allah has destined to exist, but will surely come into existence."

Bukhari 77.600

Abu Sirma said to Abu Sa'id al Khadri (Allah be pleased with him):

0 Abu Sa'id, did you hear Allah's Messenger (may peace be upon him) mentioning al-'azl?

He said: Yes, and added: We went out with Allah's Messenger (may peace be upon him) on the expedition to the Bi'l- Mustaliq and took captive some excellent Arab women; and we desired them, for we were suffering from the absence of our wives, (but at the same time) we also desired ransom for them.

So we decided to have sexual intercourse with them but by observing 'azl (Withdrawing the male sexual organ before emission of semen to avoid conception).

But we said: We are doing an act whereas Allah's Messenger is amongst us; why not ask him?

So we asked Allah's Messenger (may peace be upon him), and he said: It does not matter if you do not do it, for every soul that is to be born up to the Day of Resurrection will be born.

Imam Muslim 8:3371

As reported by the BBC, the Prophet's views on coitus interruptus and by extension contraception have encouraged "more conservative Islamic leaders have [to] openly campaigned against the use of condoms or other birth control methods, thus making population planning in many countries ineffective."

While a majority of Islamic Schools of Law allow contraceptives within a marriage setting, all are against men having a vasectomy or women a tubal ligation for this would be interfering with Allah's right to schedule a pregnancy at some point in the future.

Greetings and the Booty

> 4:86 And when you are greeted with a certain greeting, greet back with a better one or return it; for Allah keeps count of everything!

> 4:94 O believers, if you journey in the Way of Allah, be discerning and do not say to him who greets you: "You are not a believer", seeking the fleeting goods of the present life. For with Allah are abundant gains. This is how you were before and Allah has been gracious to you; so discern well. Allah is indeed fully aware of what you do!

> **Moududi:**

> In the early days of Islam the greeting as-salam 'alaykum ('peace be on you') was a distinguishing symbol of the Muslims. When a Muslim greeted another Muslim with this expression it signified that he was a member of the same community... from whom he need entertain no fear of hostility and towards whom, in return, he should not behave with hostility.

[This caused a problem] on the battlefield. Whenever a Muslim was in danger of being harmed inadvertently by other Muslims during the fighting, he resorted to either the Islamic greeting (as-salam 'alaykum) or the Islamic creed There is no god save Allah' (ili-Jl^y) in order to indicate that he was their brother-in-faith. The Muslims, however, often suspected this to be merely a ruse of the enemy and therefore sometimes disregarded the utterance of the Islamic greeting or of the Islamic creed, and killed such people and seized their belongings as booty.

"... God solved the problem by revelation. The purport of the verse is that no one has the right summarily to judge those who profess to be Muslims, and assume them to be lying for fear of their lives ... The error of letting an unbeliever go unpunished is preferable to that of killing a true believer.

The correct words to save your life!

Narrated Ibn Umar:

The Prophet sent (an army unit under the command of) Khalid bin Al-Walid to fight against the tribe of Bani Jadhima and those people could not express themselves by saying, "Aslamna (we profess Islam)," but they said, "Saba'na! Saba'na!"

Khalid kept on killing some of them and taking some others as captives, and he gave a captive to everyone of us and ordered everyone of us to kill his captive ...

Bukhari 89.299

Conscientious Objectors

Some of the early believers, "those in whose heart" Allah said "is a sickness" did not care for *fighting surahs* that demanded that they go to war and kill to advance His Kingdom on earth.

> 47:20 The believers say: "If only a surah is sent down", but when a sound surah is sent down and fighting is mentioned therein, you will see those in whose heart is a sickness look at you like one who has fainted in the throes of death. Far better for them,

> 47:21 Would have been obedience and a fair word! So when the matter is resolved, it would have been better for them to be true to Allah.

Others were worried that if they gave the Prophet too much power, he would do what Allah accuses the unbelievers of doing all the time; that is, "spread corruption in the land".

> 47:22 Would you, perhaps, if you were to rule, spread corruption in the land and sever the bonds of your kin?

> 47:23 Such are those whom Allah has cursed, and has made them deaf and blotted out their eyesight.

> 47:24 Will they not ponder the Qur'an, or are there locks upon their hearts?

In so many verses Allah reveals that it is He who causes unbelief. In the case of those I call *conscientious objectors*, it is Satan who causes former believers to abandon the faith – as far as Allah is concerned – after the *fighting surahs* have been revealed and they chose to ignore them.

> 47:25 Surely, those who have turned upon their heels after the Guidance was manifested to them, it was Satan who insinuated to them and delude them.

Conscientious Objectors

87

> 47:26 That is because they said to those who disliked what Allah has sent down: "We shall obey you in part of the matter", but Allah knows their secretiveness.

These conscientious objectors, like so many others who did not show the proper respect for Allah's revelations will be snatched by angels on Judgement Day and flown directly to Hell, and beaten on the buttocks during transit before being dropped into the Fire.

> 47:27 How, then, will it be when the angels shall carry them off, beating their faces and their buttocks?

> 47:28 That is because they have followed what has angered Allah and were averse to His good pleasure. So He has foiled their works.

Allah will disclose the name of these conscientious objectors, but who they are will obviously be revealed on the eve of any battle, or earlier, probably by the objections to going to war that they will raise, "their distorted speech", revelation 47:30 .

> 47:29 Or do those in whose hearts is a sickness think that Allah will not bring their rancours (sic) to light.

> 47:30 Had We wished, We would have shown them to you, so that you might know them by their mark. And you shall surely know them by their distorted speech. Allah knows your works.

> 47:31 And We shall test you so as to know who are the fighters among you and who are the steadfast, and we shall test your news (ascertain about you, *Moududi*).

These conscientious objectors, like conscientious objectors in any war, will have an influence, but they will not have any impact on Allah's War against the unbelievers.

> 47:32 Indeed, those who have disbelieved and barred (men) from Allah's Path and were at odds with the Messenger, after the Guidance became manifest to them, will not cause Allah any harm, and He will foil their works.

Allah will not forgive the conscientious objectors should they die *before returning to the faith*. This was war and the Prophet needed all the soldiers he could get. This may explain Allah making an exception for the conscientious objectors who were, for all intents and purposes, heretics or apostates. Apostates ordinarily cannot return to the faith and must be put to death on the spot.

> 47:33 O believers, obey Allah and obey the Messenger and do not render your actions vain.
>
> 47:34 Indeed, those who have disbelieved and barred from Allah's Path, then died as unbelievers, Allah will not forgive them.

Then there are those who do not spend enough in support of the war effort; but I digress. In the following revelations Allah uses a word to describe this lack of monetary commitment to His Cause that is controversial "because of its phonetic similarity to the racial slur nigger" although, "etymologically the two words are unrelated." Allah, of course, is not a god to shy away from controversy.

> 47:37 Were He to ask you for them and press you, you will surely be niggardly, and he will bring your rancours (sic) to light.
>
> 47:38 There you are; you are called upon to spend freely in Allah's Cause, but some of you are niggardly. Yet he who is niggardly is only niggardly unto himself. Allah is the All-Sufficient and you are the destitute. If you turn back, He will replace you by a people other than you, and they will not be like you at all.
>
> ----
>
> 3:180 And let not those who are niggardly in spending what God has given them of His Bounty suppose that it is good for them. No, it is evil; they shall carry what they stinted around their necks on the Day of Resurrection. And to Allah belongs the inheritance of the heavens and the earth. Allah is Aware of what you do!
>
> 4:39 And what would it cost them were they to believe in Allah and the Last Day and spend part of what Allah has provided for them? Allah knows them very well!
>
> 17:100 Say: "Even if you possess the treasures of My Lord's Mercy, you would still withhold them for fear of spending." Man has ever been niggardly.

War, the Life-Giver

The verse about war as a life-giver, revelation 8:24, the implication being that life really begins in the Hereafter i.e. once you are dead, was revealed during or a short time after the Battle of Badr, the first battle between the Meccans and the believers which would mark the beginning of the Arab civil war. The war would end with the Prophet in almost absolute control of the entire Arabian Peninsula.

> 8:24 O believers, respond to Allah and to the Messenger if he calls you to that which will give you life; and know that Allah stands between a man and his heart, and that unto Him you shall be gathered.
>
> 8:25 And fear a calamity which will not only afflict the wrongdoers among you; and know that Allah is Severe in retribution.
>
> 8:26 And remember when you were few and were deemed weak in the land, fearing that the people will snatch you away; but He gave you a shelter[18], strengthened you with His support and provided you with the good things[19], that perchance you may give thanks.

Life in the Hereafter is even better than life in the here-and-now complete with wealth and children.

> 8:27 O you who believe, do not betray Allah and the Messenger, nor betray your trusts knowingly.

---

[18] The reference is to the oasis city of Medina where the Prophet and his followers took refuge after being driven out of Mecca. It is from Medina that God's Messenger launched raids against the Meccan caravans passing between the city and the Red Sea which ignited an Arab civil of which the battle of Badr was the first major engagement.

[19] The good things being the plunder from the raids on the Meccan caravans.

8:28 And know that your wealth and your children are a temptation, and with Allah is a great reward.

Allah promises those who fear that what He and His Messenger are asking them to do is wrong, that, not only will He provide them with the means to know the difference between right and wrong, but also absolve them of any sins and forgive them should they die fighting on His and His Messenger's behalf.

8:29 O you who believe, if you fear Allah, He will provide you with a criteria [to distinguish right from wrong], and absolve you from your sins and forgive you. Allah's Bounty is great.

Sedition, A New Definition

It was at the battle of Badr, or shortly thereafter that Allah added to the definition of sedition, as including individuals who would take a religion other than Islam.

8:38 Say to those who disbelieve (including Abu Sufyan, the Meccan leader, and his companions): "If the desist, He will forgive them what is already done; but if they go back, then [they should remember] what befell those before them."

8:39 And fight them, so that sedition might end and the only religion will be that of Allah. Then, if they desist, Allah is fully aware of what they do.

8:40 But if they turn away, then know that Allah is your Protector; and what an Excellent Protector and Supporter He is!

GENESIS

48:28 It is He Who sent forth His Messenger with the guidance and the religion of truth, that He may exalt it above every other religion. Allah suffices as Witness.

A civil war was the genesis for the on-going bloody wars to exalt Islam above every other religion. It was a nasty business as civil wars tend to be. In civil wars kin will kill or injure kin, and the Arab civil war was no different, except that a god, a vengeful pitiless god took a personal interest in the conflict. This was to be expected, after all the war was about Him.

The Enemy Within

The Arab civil war would expand into an all-out war against all unbelievers wherever they might be. Allah, early on in the conflict established who His enemies were, making sure to single out the enemy within.

The list He established then is as valid today as it was when the Prophet was in charge of day-to-day combat operations. You see its impact in the indiscriminate killing of non-combatants such as women and children by suicide bombers. Your children, your spouses, your parents were not to be spared the homicidal hatred Allah instilled in His servants, as a Bounty and a Favour, if they did not agree to worship the One and only God. You cannot separate the hatred for unbelief from hatred of the unbeliever, and I am sure the All-Wise was aware of that.

> 49:7 Know that Allah's Messenger is in your midst. Were he to obey you in much of your affairs (*take your advice*), you would suffer hardship; but Allah has endeared belief to you and embellished it in your hearts, and He has made you to hate unbelief, sin and disobedience. Such are the rightly guided.
>
> 49:8 As a Bounty from Allah and a Favour. Allah is All-Knowing and Wise.

Kinsmen, Parents and Children

What about children? Allah will not spare the innocent in the Hereafter, so don't spare them in the here-and-now if you don't want to join your progeny in Hell, revelations 60:3-14:15.

THE WOMAN TESTED

60 Al-Mumtahanah

*In the Name of Allah,
the Compassionate, the Merciful*

60:1 O believers, do not take My enemy and your enemy for supporters, showing them friendship, when they have disbelieved what has come to you for the Truth. They expel the Messenger and expel you because you have believed in Allah, your Lord. If you have gone out to struggle in My Cause and to seek My Good Pleasure secretly showing them friendship, while I know very well what you conceal and what you reveal. He who does that among you has surely strayed from the Right Path.

60:2 If they come upon you, they will be enemies of yours and will stretch out their hands and tongues against you with malice, and they wish that you would disbelieve.

60:3 Your kinsmen or your children will not profit you on the Day of Resurrection. He shall separate you one from the other; and Allah perceives well what you do.

Allah's poster-child for hating your own flesh and blood, your wives and distant and close relations who disbelieved is Abraham, who disowned his own father.

9:114 Abraham asked forgiveness for his father, only because of a promise he had made to him; but when it became clear to him that he was an enemy of Allah, he disowned him. Indeed Abraham was compassionate, forbearing.[20]

---

[20] How the likes of Abraham's father will be dealt with on Judgement Day. When it comes to sadistic practices Allah, indeed, has no equal.

Narrated Abu Huraira:

The Prophet said, "On the Day of Resurrection Abraham will meet his father Azar whose face will be dark and covered with dust. (The Prophet Abraham will say to him): 'Didn't I tell you not to disobey me?'

His father will reply: 'Today I will not disobey you.'

Abraham will say: 'O Lord! You promised me not to disgrace me on the Day of Resurrection; and what will be more disgraceful to me than cursing and dishonoring my father?'

> 60:4 You have had a good example in Abraham and those with him, when they said to their people: "We are quit of you and what you worship apart from Allah. We disbelieve in you. Enmity and hatred have arisen between you and us forever, till you believe in Allah alone; except for Abraham's word to his father: 'I will ask forgiveness for you, although I have no power from Allah to do anything for you.' Lord, in You we trust, to you we turn and unto you is the ultimate resort.
>
> 60:5 "Lord, do not cause us to be a temptation for those who have disbelieved, and forgive us. Our Lord, You are indeed the All-Mighty, the All-Wise."
>
> 60:6 You have indeed in them a good example; that is for whoever hopes for Allah and the Last Day. Whoever repents, surely Allah is the All-Mighty, All-Praiseworthy.

The enemy within!

> 64:14 O believers, in the midst of your wives and children, there is an enemy of yours, so beware of them. Yet, if you pardon, overlook and forgive, surely Allah is forgiving, All-Merciful.

Moududi:

> [One meaning] relates to those special circumstances which most of the Muslims were facing at the time these verses were sent down, and today also they are faced by every person who embraces Islam in a non-Muslim society. At that time in Makkah and in other parts of Arabia a situation that was commonly being experienced was that a man would embrace Islam, but his wife and children would not

---

> Then Allah will say (to him):' 'I have forbidden Paradise for the disbelievers."
>
> Then he will be addressed, 'O Abraham! Look! What is underneath your feet?'
>
> He will look and there he will see a Dhabh (an animal,) blood-stained, which will be caught by the legs and thrown in the (Hell) Fire."
>
> *Bukhari 55.569*

only be disinclined to accept it but would try their best to press him to give up Islam ...

Then, it is said: "Beware of them." That is, "You should not ruin your eternal life for the sake of their worldly life."

64:15 Your possessions and children are surely a temptation, and with Allah is a great reward.

64:16 So, fear Allah as much as you can, listen, obey and spend freely (*in the Cause of Allah*). That is best for you. He who is guarded against the avarice of his soul – those are the prosperous.

Women Choose Sides

The wives of Meccan men were not prisoners in their husband's household. They accompanied their husbands to war; any fighting was also about them – mainly about them in the Arab civil war as it would turn out – therefore they exposed themselves to many of the same risks. They urged their husbands on from the sidelines all the while shouting insults at the enemy. Not the shy retiring type; at the battle of Uhud, which was one of the few battles the Meccans won, many of them stripped to the waist giving their husbands a clear indication of what and for whom they were fighting.

Many of these women must have left their husband when their partner joined the religion which considered them no more than chattel to be bartered between believing men for Allah to send a revelation that the husbands whose wives deserted them should be compensated.

60:11 If any of your wives desert you to the unbelievers, and you decide to penalize them, then give those [husbands] whose wives have gone away the like of what they have spent (*the dowry*), and fear Allah in whom you believe.

Why would such women become believers, which of course some did? Allah rightly questioned their loyalty and motives and demanded that their faith be tested. In the same revelation He established that a believing female could never be married to an unbeliever.

60:10 O believers, if believing women come to you as

Emigrants, then test them; Allah knows better their faith. If you find them to be believers, do not send them back to the unbelievers. They are neither lawful to the unbelieving men, nor are those men lawful to them. Give them what they [the unbelieving husbands] had paid in dowry; and you are not at fault if you marry them, provided you pay them their dowries. Do not hold fast to unbelieving women; demand what you have spent and let them demand what they have spent. That is Allah's Judgement. He judges between you, and Allah is All-Knowing and Wise.

Battle of Badr

The Prophet and his followers, after being run out of Mecca, took refuge in Medina from which they attacked the caravans passing between the Red Sea and the oasis city on their way to and from Mecca, igniting a civil war.

> **Narrated Jabir:**
>
> The Prophet sent us as an army unit of three hundred warriors under the command of Abu Ubaida to ambush a caravan of the Quraish ...
>
> *Bukhari 67.402*

The first real battle of what would become a bloody fratricidal war was an attack on a force of an estimated one thousands Meccans sent to protect a large caravan which the Muslims intended to plunder. The Prophet, initially, wanted to attack the caravan before the Meccan forces could intervene, but Allah promised him a victory no matter which he chose to attack. With God's guarantee of victory, His Messenger decided on the Meccan armed detachment, a decision which did not meet with unanimous approval.

> 8:5 Just as when your (meaning Muhammad) Lord brought you out in truth from your house (*to fight*)[21], though a group of the believers disliked it.
>
> 8:6 They disputed with you concerning the Truth after it had become manifest, as though they were being led to their deaths while looking on.
>
> 8:7 And [remember] how Allah promised you that one of the two [enemy] groups (the Meccan caravan of the

---

[21] Moududi quotes a different translation where it's all about the spoils:

> 8:5 (Now with regard to the spoils the same situation exists as when) your Lord brought you forth from your home in a righteous cause while a party among the believers were much averse to it.

Quraysh and the army which was sent to defend it) would be yours, and you wanted the unarmed one (the caravan) to be yours. Allah, however, willed the Truth to triumph in accordance with His Words and to cut off the remnants of the unbelievers.

> 8:8 So that He may cause the Truth to triumph and nullify falsehood, even though the wicked sinner dislike it.

To avoid His Messenger getting cold feet the night before the battle, in a dream Allah made the enemy appear to be much fewer and repeated the same illusion the next day to a fully awake Prophet.

> 8:43 [Remember] when Allah showed them [O Muhammad] in your sleep as few. Had He showed them to you as many, you would have lost heart and you would have differed over the matter. But Allah saved you. He knows what is hidden in the hearts.

> 8:44 And [remember] when He showed them to you, as you met, few in your eyes, and made you few in their eyes; so that Allah might bring about a matter already decreed. And unto Allah shall all matters return.

If only the Prophet was subjected to the illusion of a small Meccan army, then the following verse, where the believers saw themselves outnumbered two to one[22], makes sense:

> 3:13 There surely was a sign for you in the two armies that confronted each other (at the Battle of Badr); the one side fighting for the cause of Allah, and the others consisting of unbelievers. The believers saw them with their very eyes to be twice their actual number. God will strengthen with His Might whomever He pleases. Surely, there is in this a lesson for those who are possessed of vision.

No matter their relative strength, the believers held the high ground.

---

[22] The Mohsin Khan translation disputes Allah's estimate, making it 3 to 1, and the sign was for the Jews.

> 3:13 There has already been a sign for you (O Jews) in the two armies that met (in combat i.e. the Battle of Badr). One was fighting in the Cause of Allah, and as for the other, (they) were disbelievers. They (the believers) saw them (the disbelievers) with their own eyes twice their number (although they were thrice their number). And Allah supports with His Victory whom He wills. Verily, in this is a lesson for those who understand.

They would have abandoned that strategic position and attacked the caravan ("cavalcade" in revelation 8:42), with disastrous result had Allah not already decided how the battle should unfold.

> 8:42 While you were on the nearer side [of the valley] and they were on the farther side, with the cavalcade beneath you. Had you made an appointment, you would surely have failed to keep the appointment. But [this happened] so that Allah might bring about a matter already decreed, and that those who were to perish would perish after a clear proof [had been given], and those who were to survive would survive after a clear proof [had been given]. And surely Allah is All-Hearing, All-Knowing.

The Muslim defeated the Meccans at the famous battle of Badr with Allah taking credit for the victory. And why shouldn't He. After all, He did send an army of invisible angels to help the Muslims defeat their enemy, and made it possible for the believers to fall asleep, in a atypical rain, the night before the battle.

> 8:9 And when you called upon your Lord for help, He answered you: "I will re-enforced you with a thousand angels following one another."

> 8:10 Allah did this only as good tidings and that your hearts might be assured thereby. Victory comes only from Allah; Allah is indeed Mighty and Wise.

> 8:11 [Remember] when He allowed slumber to overcome you as an assurance from Him, and sent you water down from heaven so as to purify you, relieve you of the Devil's temptation, fortify your hearts and steady your feet therewith.

Words of encouragement for His angels:

> 8:12 And when your Lord revealed to the angels: "I am with you; so support those who believe. I will cast terror into the hearts of those who disbelieve; so strike upon the necks and strike every fingertip of theirs."

> 8:13 That is because they opposed Allah and His Messenger; and he who opposes Allah and His Messenger [will find] Allah's Punishment very severe.

> 8:14 This is how it will be; so taste it; the torture of the Fire is awaiting the unbelievers.

Words of encouragement for the believers:

> 8:15 O believers, if you meet the unbelievers on the march, do not turn your backs upon them.
>
> 8:16 Whoever turns his back on that day, unless preparing to resume fighting, or joining another group, incurs Allah's Wrath and his refuge is Hell; and what an evil fate!
>
> ----
>
> 8:45 O believers, if you encounter an enemy host, stand fast and remember Allah frequently, that perchance you may prosper.
>
> 8:46 And obey Allah and His Messenger and do not quarrel among yourselves lest you lose heart and your strength dissipates. And stand fast, for Allah is on the side of those who stand fast.
>
> 8:47 And do not be like those who went out of their homes boastfully showing off in front of the people[23], while they barred others from the Path of Allah. Allah is fully aware of what they do.

Words of encouragement from Satan for the unbelievers. The Devil fled the battlefield before any actual engagement, which probably demoralized the opponents of the believers somewhat.

> 8:48 And the Devil made their [foul] deeds look fair to them saying: "No man shall overcome you today; and I am indeed by your side." But when the two hosts sighed each other, he turned on his heels saying: "I am quit of you; I see what you do not see; I fear Allah, and Allah is stern in retribution."

What about the hypocrites?

> 8:49 And the hypocrites and those in whose hearts is a sickness said: "Their religion has mislead those people (the

---

[23] "This alludes to the army of the disbelieving Quraysh, which, when it proceeded on a military expedition against the Muslims, was accompanied by singing and dancing minstrels." *Moududi*

Muslims)." But he who trusts in Allah will find Allah is Mighty and Wise.

Strong winds lashed the battlefield. One wind blast, the Prophet told his fighters, was one thousand angels led by the archangel Gabriel coming to their aid[24]. The next blast, he said, was another thousand angels led by the archangel Michael. A third was still another thousand angels led by the archangel Saraphel. Allah gives details of this re-enforcement from heaven, but not before reminding the faithful of the second encounter between the Muslims and the Meccans at the Battle of Uhud (March 19, 625).

> 3:123 Allah had already given you victory at Badr, at a time when you were still powerless; so fear Allah that perchance you might thankful!
>
> 3:124 When you were telling the believers: "Is it not enough that your Lord should reinforce you with three thousand angels sent down?"

Even with the assistance of three thousand angels, the Prophet's men could not defeat the Meccans. Allah had to send another two thousand angels (unless these angels were held in reserve and the battle was won without their assistance), bringing the total number of winged combatants the Almighty committed to the Battle of Badr to five thousand.

---

[24] Gabriel was proud of the way his angels fought, and he may also have been the only mounted warrior at the battle of Badr.

Narrated Rifaa: (who was one of the Badr warriors)

Gabriel came to the Prophet and said, "How do you look upon the warriors of Badr among yourselves?"

The Prophet said, "As the best of the Muslims." or said a similar statement.

On that, Gabriel said, "And so are the Angels who participated in the Badr (battle)."

Bukhari 59.327

Narrated Ibn Abbas:

The Prophet said on the day (of the battle) of Badr, "This is Gabriel holding the head of his horse and equipped with arms for the battle.

Bukhari 59.330

> 3:125 Yes, if you forbear and fear Allah and the enemy attack you at once, Your Lord will reinforce you with five thousand marked angels.
>
> 3:126 Allah has not intended this except as good news to you and that your hearts might be reassured thereby. Victory comes only from Allah, the Mighty, the Wise!

The angels were not only there to fight, but also to carry the souls of the dead unbelievers to Hell.

> 8:50 And if you could only see when the angels carry off the unbelievers, striking their faces and their rears [saying]: "Taste the punishment of the Fire."
>
> 8:51 That is on account of what you have done, and Allah is not unjust to His servants.

The total number of enemy dead at the Battle of Badr was 70[25]. And as Allah reminds the believers, it was not they who slew them.

> 8:17 It was not you (those addressed are the Muslims) who slew them, but Allah; and when you (Muhammad) threw (he pebbles or a handful of dust at the enemy in retaliation) it was actually Allah who threw; so that He might generously reward the believers. Allah is All-Hearing, All-Knowing.

Why Allah threw the dust:

> 8:18 That was done, so that Allah might foil the machinations of the unbelievers.

Allah is on the side of the believers, even if it is not obvious until the very last statement in the following revelation.

> 8:19 If you seek victory, the victory has been granted you; and if you desist, it will be better for you; but if you come back, We will come back (We will again support the

---

[25] **Narrated Al-Bara' bin 'Azib**:

On the day of Uhud the Prophet appointed 'Abdullah bin Jubair as chief of the archers, and seventy among us were injured and martyred. On the day (of the battle) of Badr, the Prophet and his companions had inflicted 140 casualties on the pagans, 70 were taken prisoners, and 70 were killed ..."

Bukhari 56.322

believers) and your forces will avail you nothing, however numerous they are. Allah is on the side of the believers.

The Prophet had one of his most vocal critics, the poet al-Nadr whom he spotted after the battle, killed on the spot, but he did show mercy to sixty or more other prisoners. He ignored demands that each be killed by a relative to avoid a blood feud and a demand that they be burnt alive, and ordered that they be ransomed. He was exercising Allah's prerogative.

> 3:127 That He may cut off a group of the unbelievers or humiliate them, so that they may turn away completely baffled.
>
> 3:128 It is no business of yours whether Allah forgives them or punishes them; for they are indeed evil-doers!

What Pharaoh's people and the dead unbelievers at Badr had in common:

> 8:52 Just like the wont of Pharaoh's people and those who preceded them; they disbelieved in their Lord's Revelations; so Allah punished them for their sins. Allah is Strong and Stern in retribution.
>
> 8:53 That is because Allah never changes a favour He confers on a people unless they change what is in their hearts, and because Allah is All-Hearing, All-Knowing.
>
> 8:54 Just like the wont of Pharaoh's people and those who preceded them; they denied Allah's revelations, so We destroyed them because of their sins and We drowned Pharaoh's people. They were all wrongdoers.

None of the victorious warriors of the battle of Badr survived the upheaval that followed the assassination of the second and third Caliph.

Narrated Said bin Al-Musaiyab:

> When the first civil strife (in Islam) took place because of the murder of Uthman, it left none of the Badr warriors alive.
>
> When the second civil strife, that is the battle of Al-Harra, took place, it left none of the Hudaibiya treaty companions alive.

Then the third civil strife took place and it did not subside till it had exhausted all the strength of the people.

Bukhari 59.358

Sparrows at War

The Koran does mention another A.D. confrontation in which Allah spectacularly interfered with the outcome. In this battle He did not send angels to defeat His enemies but sparrows. The following story about birds defeating an army on elephants is from Virgil Gheorghiu's *La vie de Mahomet*, with supporting verses from the Koran.

The inhabitants of the Arab Peninsula knew that Mecca was special to God even before the Prophet made it official. It is reported in the *Traditions* that in 570, the year of Muhammad's birth, Abraha, the Christian ruler of the principality of Saba' in Yemen (then part of the Abyssinian Empire) marched on Mecca after the Meccans allegedly tried to burn down a church he had built and which the Meccans feared would attract more converts to Christianity.

On the approach to Mecca the elephant Abraha was ridding stopped and knelt on the ground and refused to go any further. Suddenly, out of the sky appeared squadron after squadron of Sparrows armed with tiny stones with which they bombed the army of Abraha killing all the estimated 60,000 men, their elephants, camels and horses.

As an example of how pre-Islamic mythology made its way into the Koran, one of the last surahs is dedicated to this unlikely encounter of which history has no record.

THE ELEPHANT

105 Al-Fîl

*In the Name of Allah,
the Compassionate, the Merciful*

105:1 Have you not seen how your Lord dealt with the Companions of the Elephant?

105:2 Did he not turn their cunning into perdition?

105:3 And send upon them swarms of birds;

105:4 Hurling upon them stones of clay;

105:5 And so He reduced them to munched blades of grass.

Spoils of Badr

Dead pagans down the well and booty for the believers. What a God!

Narrated Ibn Shihab:

These were the battles of Allah's Apostle (which he fought), and while mentioning (the Badr battle) he said, while the corpses of the pagans were being thrown into the well, Allah's Apostle said (to them), "Have you found what your Lord promised true?"

Abdullah said, "Some of the Prophet's companions said, "O Allah's Apostle! You are addressing dead people.'"

Allah's Apostle replied, "You do not hear what I am saying, better than they."

The total number of Muslim fighters from Quraish who fought in the battle of Badr and were given their share of the booty, were 81 men."

Az-Zubair said, "When their shares were distributed, their number was 101 men. But Allah knows it better."

Bukhari 59.360

Christianity was well established on the Arabian Peninsula thanks, in part, to the pioneering efforts of one of the original apostles, Bartholomew. After the battle there are the spoils and a discussion ensues as to who gets what. Those who are familiar with Jesus' response in the Gospel of Luke to the question posed by the scribes "Is it lawful for us to give tribute to Caesar, or not?" will see a similarity in the Prophet's response to the question of "Who gets what?" The big difference being that God's Messenger as Allah's Overseer on earth is entitled to both Allah's and Caesar's share.

THE SPOILS

8 Al-Anfâl

In the Name of Allah,
the Compassionate, the Merciful

8:1 They ask you about the spoils (taken by the Muslims

after the Battle of Badr), say: "The spoils belong to Allah and to the Messenger. So fear Allah and settle your differences." Obey Allah and His Messenger if you are true believers.

But there is of course more to being a believer than simply being entitled to an unbeliever's possessions, as Allah quickly reminds those whose mind is focussed on the booty.

> 8:2 The true believers are whose hearts, upon the mention of Allah, quiver with fear; and when His Revelations are recited to them, they strengthen their faith. They put their trust in their Lord.
>
> 8:3 Those who perform the prayer, and spend of what We provided for them.
>
> 8:4 Those are in truth the believers; they shall enjoy with their Lord a high station and receive forgiveness and a generous provision.

Allah in a subsequent revelation opts for a more even-handed distribution of the booty.

> 8:41 And know that whatever booty you take, the fifth thereof is for Allah, the Messenger, the near of kin, the orphan and the wayfarer, if you really believe in Allah and in what We revealed to our Servant on the day of decision (the Battle of Badr), the day when the two hosts met. Allah has power over everything.

This did not, however, stop the grumbling about how the alms were distributed.

> 9:58 And some of them disparage your handling of the alms. If they are given part of it they are satisfied, but if they are not given any, they turn away angrily.
>
> 9:59 And would that they were satisfied with what Allah and His Messenger gave them and said: "Allah suffices us; Allah will give us of His Bounty, as will His Messenger. We turn humbly to Him."

The dissatisfaction may have had to the with the wealth which the Prophet spent in "Allah's Way" which as Allah explains in revelation

9:60 is a legitimate charitable expense. It costs a lot of money to maintain an army fighting in Allah's Path.

> 9:60 The alms are for the poor, the needy, their collectors and those whose hearts are bound together[26], as well as for the freeing of slaves, [repaying] the debtors, spending in Allah's Path, and for the wayfarer. Thus Allah commands. Allah is All-Knowing, Wise.

---

[26] "'those whose hearts are to be won over' A portion of Zakat Funds may also be given to win over to Islam those who might be engaged in anti-Islamic activities or to those in the camp of the unbelievers who might be brought to help the Muslims or to those newly converted Muslims, who might be inclined to revert to kufr if no monetary help was extended to them. It is permissible to award pensions to them or give them lump sums of money to make them helpers of Islam or submissive to it or at least to render them into harmless enemies." *Moududi*

Battle of Uhud

Narrated Al-Bara bin Azib:

The Prophet appointed Abdullah bin Jubair as the commander of the infantry men (archers) who were fifty on the day (of the battle) of Uhud. He instructed them, "Stick to your place, and don't leave it even if you see birds snatching us, till I send for you; and if you see that we have defeated the infidels and made them flee, even then you should not leave your place till I send for you."

Then the infidels were defeated.

By Allah, I saw the women fleeing lifting up their clothes revealing their leg-bangles and their legs. So, the companions of Abdullah bin Jubair said, "The booty! O people, the booty! Your companions have become victorious, what are you waiting for now?"

Abdullah bin Jubair said, "Have you forgotten what Allah's Apostle said to you?"

They replied, "By Allah! We will go to the people (i.e. the enemy) and collect our share from the war booty." But when they went to them, they were forced to turn back defeated ...

Bukhari 52.276

The believers were well on their way to winning their second encounter with the Meccans – this battle taking place on the slopes and flats of Mount Uhud – when the Muslim archers left the battle early, thinking it was already won, to be the first to plunder the undefended Meccan camp. The Meccan cavalry counter-attacked, seriously wounding the Prophet and routing the Muslim forces. Had they pressed on, they would have completely crushed the believers. Revelations 3:121-122 are about this near-disaster at Uhud which

Allah initially takes credit for averting by His *moral* support of the two battalions commanded by His Messenger.

> 3:121 [And remember] when you (Muhammad) went at daybreak, away from your family, in order to lead the believers to their battle stations (at the Battle of Uhud); Allah is All-Hearing, All-Knowing!
>
> 3:122 Two of your battalions[27] were about to lose heart, and Allah was their Protector. In Allah let the believers put their trust!

The lure of the booty overwhelmed the need to keep on killing. How the near-disaster unfolded and what happened next, in Allah's own words.

> 3:152 Allah fulfilled His Promise to you when, by His Leave, you went on killing them; until you lost heart and dissented about the affair and disobeyed (the Muslims were victorious until the archers disobeyed the Prophet's orders), after He had shown you what you cherished. Some of you desired this world (left their position to get a share of the booty), others the Hereafter. Then, He turned you away from them (the Qurashite foes of the Muslims) in order to test you, and He has forgiven you. Allah is Gracious to the believers!

Even with the departure of the archers, the Muslims might still have been able to withstand the renewed assault of the Meccans if someone by the name of Suraqah had not shouted that the Prophet, who had been wounded in the encounter, was dead, causing consternation in the believers' ranks and prompting many to flee in disarray in what became a rout.

> 3:153 [Remember] how you fled and paid heed to no one, while the Messenger was calling you from the rear. Thus He rewarded you with grief upon grief, lest you should not be sorry for what you missed or what befell you. Allah is Aware of what you do!

After the grief, whatever it was, Allah caused some who could still not be trusted in battle, "as a security" to fall asleep, and still others to

---

[27] "They belonged to Banu Salamah and Banu Harithah who formed the two wings of the Muslim army which was led by the Prophet" *Fakhry*

express doubts about what they were fighting for and was it worth risking their lives, thereby providing Allah with an opportunity for rebuttal.

> 3:154 Then He sent down upon you, after the grief, as a security, slumber overcoming a group of you, whereas another group were only concerned about themselves, entertaining untrue thoughts about Allah, like the thoughts of the pagans. They say: "Do we have any part in the affair?" Say: "The whole affair is Allah's." They conceal in their hearts what they do not reveal to you. They say: "Had we had any part in the affair, we would not have been killed here." Say: "Had you been in your homes, those who were destined to be killed would have sallied forth to the places where they would be slain; so that Allah might purify what is in your hearts. Allah knows well what is hidden in the breasts."

Suraqah would deny, until his dying day, that he was the one who shouted that God's Messenger had been killed. Allah did not blame him, He blamed the Devil.

> 3:155 Those of you, who fled on the day the two armies met, were made to slip by the Devil, on account of something they had done. However, Allah has forgiven them; Allah is indeed Forgiving and Merciful.

Don't be like the unbelievers and think that you can escape death by playing it safe.

> 3:156 O believers, do not be like the unbelievers, who say about their brethren when they [die] while travelling abroad or fighting: "Had they stayed with us, they would not have died or been killed." Allah wished to make that a cause of anguish in their hearts. It is Allah who causes men to live and die, and Allah has Knowledge of what you do!

Dying fighting for Allah is much better than whatever the unbelievers can amass in this life.

> 3:157 And were you to be killed or to die in the Way of Allah, forgiveness and mercy from Allah are far better than what they amass.

A reminder that those who die fighting for Allah immediately join Him in Paradise – no life-in-the-grave waiting for Judgement day for these brave men.

> 3:158 And were you to die or to be killed, it is unto Allah that you will be gathered.

Praise for how His Messenger handled the aftermath of Uhud, and some advice.

> 3:159 It was by a mercy from Allah that you dealt leniently with them (the Muslim fighters who flinched in the midst of the battle); for had you been cruel and hard-hearted, they would have dispersed from around you. So, pardon them, ask Allah's Forgiveness for them and consult them in the conduct of affairs. Then, when you are resolved, trust in Allah; Allah indeed loves those who trust [in Him].

In Allah we trust!

> 3:160 If Allah supports you, no one will overcome you; but if He forsakes you, then who will be able to support you after Him? And in Allah let the believers put their trust!

And in the Prophet!

> 3:161 It does not benefit any Prophet to cheat [in handling the booty]; for whoever cheats will bring the fruit of his dishonesty with him on the Day of Resurrection. Then, each soul shall be paid in full for what it earned (its works); and they will not be wronged.

Who's to Blame for the Defeat?

All believers were not equal at the Battle of Uhud, and the less equal appear to have been responsible for the rout. And while God's Messenger may have forgiven those who fled the battlefield, and Allah shown a willingness to forgive and forget, His Mercy may not encompass all of those who fled the battle, even if He contrived the defeat for His own ends.

> 3:162 What, is he who follows Allah's good Pleasure like him who brings upon himself God's Wrath? Hell is his refuge, and what a wretched destiny!

3:163 They (the believers) have different grades in Allah's Sight; and Allah has knowledge of what they do!

3:164 Allah has been gracious to the believers, sending them a Messenger from among themselves to recite to them His Revelations, to purify them and to teach them the Book and the Wisdom, though they had been in manifest error before that.

3:165 And when a misfortune befell you (in the Battle of Uhud) after you had inflicted twice as much (in the Battle of Badr), you said: "Whence is this?"; say: "It is from yourselves." Surely Allah has power over everything!

3:166 And what befell you on that day the two armies met (in the Battle of Uhud) was by Allah's Leave, that He might know the true believers;

If Allah knows what is in men's hearts, was the defeat at Uhud really necessary.

3:167 And that He might know the hypocrites. When it was said to them: "Come, fight in the way of Allah or defend yourselves", they replied: "If only we knew how to fight, we would have followed you." On that day, they were closer to disbelief than to belief. They say with their tongues what is not in their hearts; and Allah knows best what they conceal!

A reminder from Allah that those who have died at the battle of Uhud are well taken care off; that the living should be so lucky.

3:169 And do not think those who have been killed in the Way of Allah as dead; they are rather living with their Lord, well provided for.

3:170 Rejoicing in what their Lord has given them of His bounty, and they rejoice for those who stayed behind and did not join them; knowing that they have nothing to fear and that they shall not grieve.

3:171 They rejoice in the Grace of Allah and His Favour, and that Allah will not withhold the reward of the faithful;

This reminder of the good life after death, was probably Allah anticipating the next encounter with the unbelievers, encouraging those who may have been spooked by the death of their comrades in faith, including the wounded, to return to the fray when called upon, if not for the rewards, than because of what He will do to them if they fail in their duty to Him and His Messenger.

> 3:172 Those who responded to Allah's Call and the Messenger's after they had incurred many wounds. To those of them who do what is right and fear Allah, a great reward is in store.
>
> 3:173 Those to whom the people said: "The people have been arrayed against you; so fear them." But this increased their faith and so they said: "Allah is Sufficient for us. He is the Best Guardian!"
>
> 3:174 Thus they came back with a Grace and a Bounty from Allah. No harm touched them; and they complied with Allah's good Pleasure. Allah's Bounty is great!
>
> 3:175 That indeed is the Devil frightening his followers; but do not fear them and fear Me, if you are true believers!

Do not grieve for your relatives who died in the Battle of Uhud. If they died as unbelievers, not only are they not deserving of your tears, but the painful death they may have just suffered is just the beginning of an eternity of pain for not believing in Allah and His Messenger.

> 3:176 And do not let those who hasten to disbelieve make you grieve. They will certainly not cause Allah any harm. Allah wishes not to give them any share in the Hereafter, and a terrible punishment awaits them!

Understood is that if they don't get a share, your share will be bigger. The unbelievers, by not believing in Allah, will not cause Him any harm and for this, they will not be welcomed in His abode, Paradise, which is understandable. What is less so, is why He wants to make them suffer for an eternity when He readily admits, again, in the very next revelation that their disbelief is innocuous.

> 3:177 Those who trade belief for disbelief will not cause Allah any harm, and a painful punishment awaits them!

As part of the lessons from the Battle of Uhud, Allah breaks the familial ties that bound the tribes for countless generations, substituting religious ties in their place. Your co-religionist are now your family and only friends, and only they are deserving of God's Mercy, and your tears. As for the relatives that survived Uhud:

> 3:178 Let the unbelievers not suppose that Our prolonging their days is better for them. We only prolong their days so that they may grow in sin, and a humbling punishment awaits them.

Returning to what the defeat at Uhud was very much about: "separating the vile from the decent".

> 3:179 Allah will not leave the faithful in the state in which you are, until He separates the vile from the decent. Nor will Allah make known to you the unseen; but Allah chooses of His Messengers whomever He pleases. Believe then in Allah and His Messengers; and if you believe and fear Allah, you will have a great reward.

~~~~~~~~~~~~~~~~~

More words of encouragement for the fighting believers, after the near disaster at Uhud:

> 3:144 Muhammad is merely a Messenger, before whom many Messengers have come and gone. If then he dies or gets killed, you will turn on your heels? Should any man turn on his heels, he will not cause Allah any harm; and Allah will reward the thankful.

> 3:145 It is not given to any soul to die, except with Allah's Leave, at a fixed time. He who desires the reward of this world, We will give him [part] of it, and he who desires the reward of the life to come, We will give him [part] of it; and We shall reward the thankful.

> 3:146 How many Prophets with whom large multitudes have fought; they were not daunted on account of what befell them in the Cause of Allah. They did not weaken or cringe; and Allah loves the steadfast!

> 3:147 Their only words were: "Lord, forgive us our sins and our excess in our affairs. Make firm our feet and grant us victory over the unbelieving people."

> 3:148 Therefore Allah granted them the reward of this life and the excellent reward (Paradise) of the life to come, and Allah loves the beneficent.

Medina

The Jews of Medina

In Medina lived three Jewish Tribes. The Jews of Medina were a wealthy, prosperous community. They were also considered the intellectual class of the city. When Muhammad sought refuge in Medina he was welcomed by the Jews, in part, because of his preaching that the god of the Old Testament was the one and only god. They even entered into a covenant with him to come to his (the Muslims) aid if he was ever attacked. In return, he signed a promise of non-aggression.

The three Jewish tribes of Medina did not see the rise of Islam as a threat to them until the Muslims developed an appetite for booty and started raiding the caravans that passed by the city on their way to and from Mecca. These raids were sanctioned by the Koran since the booty the Muslims were taking was from unbelievers.

The Muslim victory over the Meccans at Badr particularly unnerved the Jews. The Muslims at Badr defeated a much larger force dispatched by Mecca to protect a rich caravan returning from Damascus which the Prophet planned on plundering. At the Battle of Badr the Prophet not only demonstrated a unnatural blood-lust and a thirst for revenge but also may again have given some reason to question his sanity.

It was at Badr, that the Prophet first informed his followers of the concept of life in the grave. After the battle, the Muslim dead were given a proper burial while the Meccan casualties were simply thrown down a well. God's Messenger was seen shouting at the corpses in the well. This yelling at dead people left some of his followers perplexed, but the Prophet had an explanation.

Narrated Ibn Umar:

The Prophet looked at the people of the well and said, "Have you found true what your Lord promised you?"

> Somebody said to him, "You are addressing dead people."
>
> He replied, "You do not hear better than they but they cannot reply."
>
> Bukhari 23.452

But it was not questions as to the Prophet's sanity that alarmed the Jews of Medina, but what God's Messenger did after he returned victorious to their city. The victory at Badr and the prestige and wealth that came with it emboldened the Prophet to silence his most vocal and persistent critics, the poets.

The first poet to be killed was al-Nadr. The Meccans had praised his verses as superior to those of the Prophet and this had enraged the perfect human being. When God's Messenger spotted al-Nadr among the prisoners captured at Badr he had him beheaded on the spot. Next to die was the poetess Asma bint Marwan. She was stabbed to death while sleeping with an infant suckling at her breast. Next, the Jewish poet Abu Afak who was also killed while he slept.

> "He waited for an opportunity until a hot night came, and Abu Afak slept in an open place. Salim b. Umayr knew it, so he placed the sword on his liver and pressed it till it reached his bed. The enemy of Allah screamed and the people, who were his followers rushed him, took him to his house and interred him." *Ibn S'ad*

After every murder the assassin would go to the Mosque to inform God's Messenger and be praised for what they had done at his insistence. For example, the killer of Asma bint Marwan had just entered the mosque when the Prophet asked him "Have you slain the daughter of Marwan?" Ibn S'ad's on the words first spoken by "the Apostle of Allah":

> This was the word that was first heard from the Apostle of Allah, may Allah bless him. When Umayr replied that the job had been carried out with success, Muhammad said, "You have helped God and His apostle, O Umayr!"
>
> When Umayr asked if he would have to bear any evil consequences, the apostle said, "Two goats won't butt their heads about her."

Muhammad then praised Umayr in front of all gathered for prayer for his act of murder, and Umayr went back to his people.[28]

Adding to the Jews of Medina's uneasiness caused by the cold-blooded murder of the poets was a revelation the Prophet received at about this time telling him that he could effectively renounce any treaty at his discretion.

> 8:58 And should you fear treachery from any people, throw back their treaty to them in like manner. Allah does not like the treacherous.

God's Messenger was a patient man. With Allah giving him a freehand to break any non-aggression promise he had made, it was only a matter of time before an opportunity arose to use his newfound power.

After Badr the Prophet not only felt his position secure enough to have his critics silence with a dagger or a sword but also to put his newfound prestige on the line by seeking to impose a head tax, the Jizya, on the Jews and Christians. The Jews ridiculed his proposal

---

[28] The Medinan Arabs who converted to Islam, the so-called Ansar (helpers), proved particularly pitiless in depriving unbelievers of their lives and property.

Narrated Abdur-Rahman bin 'Auf:

I got an agreement written between me and Umaiya bin Khalaf that Umaiya would look after my property (or family) in Mecca and I would look after his in Medina.

When I mentioned the word Ar-Rahman' in the documents, Umaiya said, "I do not know Ar-Rahman.' Write down to me your name, (with which you called yourself) in the Pre-lslamic Period of Ignorance." So, I wrote my name 'Abdu Amr'.

On the day (of the battle) of Badr, when all the people went to sleep, I went up the hill to protect him. Bilal saw him (i.e. Umaiya) and went to a gathering of Ansar and said, "(Here he is) Umaiya bin Khalaf! Woe to me if he escapes!"

So, a group of Ansar went out with Bilal to follow us ('Abdur-Rahman and Umaiya).

Being afraid that they would catch us, I left Umaiya's son for them to keep them busy but the Ansar killed the son and insisted on following us.

Umaiya was a fat man, and when they approached us, I told him to kneel down, and he knelt, and I laid myself on him to protect him, but the Ansar killed him by passing their swords underneath me, and one of them injured my foot with his sword. (The sub narrator said, "Abdur-Rahman used to show us the trace of the wound on the back of his foot.")

Bukhari 38.498

saying that Allah could not be so poor as to require their money.

God's Messenger swallowed his pride and patiently waited for an opportunity to make the Jews pay, and pay dearly for their insolence, as was his way. An irresistible opportunity for revenge and for plunder presented itself with the retaliation killing of a Muslim by a Jew of the Banu Qaynuqa, the smallest of the three Jewish tribes of Medina. The story as told by Abul Kasem, a former Muslim and author of *A Complete Guide to Allah:*

> An Arab girl, married to a Muslim convert of Medina went to the Jewish shop of a goldsmith in the market place of Qaynuqa. While waiting for some ornaments, she sat down. A silly neighbour secretly pinned the lower hem of her skirt. When she arose, the awkward expose made everyone laugh. She screamed with shame. A passing Muslim witnessed the incident and killed the offending Jew. The brother of the Jew then killed the Muslim. The family of the murdered Muslim then appealed to the converts of Medina to take revenge.
>
> The skirmish now became general and Muhammad made no attempt to mitigate the situation, nor did he try to bring the offending parties to justice. He immediately gathered his followers under the white banner in the hand of Hamzah and marched forward to attack the Jewish tribe. The Jews took shelter in their fortified apartments. So, Muhammad laid a siege and a full blockade was imposed. The siege lasted for fifteen days... [the] Jews had no choice but to surrender to Muhammad. Their hands were tied behind their backs and preparations were made for their execution. At this time, Abd Allah ibn Ubayy ... a new convert to Islam begged Muhammad for mercy, but Muhammad turned his face away. Abd Allah persisted. Finally, Muhammad yielded and let the prisoners escape execution. He then cursed the Jews and Abd Allah ibn Ubay with Allah's punishment. Then Muhammad ordered the Jews of Banu Qaynuqa to leave Medina within three days.

After the exile of the Banu Qaynuqa the Prophet legalized the killing of Jews.

> The messenger of God said, "Whoever of the Jews falls into your hands, kill him." *Tabari*

The next to be forced out were the Banu Nadir. The Banu Nadir Jews owned large tracks of land on the outskirts of Medina on which they cultivated date palms. They too took refuge in their fortress when they ran afoul of the Prophet. Again God's Messenger besieged their fortress.

There was always a chance that the remaining Jewish tribe would come to their aid. The Muslims were not yet strong enough to withstand a concerted effort by the Jews to defend themselves, therefore the siege had to be ended as quickly as possible. To disheartened and convince the Banu Nadir that there was no future for them in Medina, even if the siege was lifted, God's Messenger ordered that all the Banu Nadir's date palms be cut down. This early version of scorched-earth warfare was taboo for both the Arabs and Jews. The Prophet justified his breaking of this long-standing prohibition with the usual revelation from Allah.

> 59:5 Whatever palm trees you cut of or leave standing upon their roots is only by Allah's Leave, and that He might disgrace the sinners.

The Prophet's share of the property of the Banu Nadir may have made some jealous.

> 59:6 Whatever spoils Allah bestows on His Messenger from them, you did not send against them any horses or other mounts; but Allah confers on His Messengers authority over whoever he pleases. Allah has power over everything.

> 59:7 And whatever spoils Allah bestows on His Messenger from the inhabitants of the cities belongs to Allah, His Messenger, the kinsmen, the orphans, the destitute and the wayfarers; so that it might not circulate among the rich of you. Whatever the Messenger gives you, take; but whatever he forbids, refrain from. Fear Allah, for Allah is terrible in retribution.

Do unto others as was done to you? Part of the plunder from the siege of the Banu Nadir went to the emigrants from Mecca, and another to supporters in Medina.

> 59:8 Give to the poor Emigrants who were driven out of their homes and their possessions, seeking bounty from Allah and good pleasure and assisting Allah and His Messenger. Those indeed are the truthful ones.

> 59:9 And those who had already established themselves and embraced their Faith before them (the people of Medina known as al-Ansar or supporters, as against the Meccans known as al-Muhajirun, or emigrants) love those who emigrated to them; and they do not find in their hearts any need for what had been bestowed upon them and prefer them to themselves, even if they are in dire need. He is indeed prosperous who is guarded against the avarice of his soul.

The spoils from the dispossession of the Badu Nadir, as are the spoils from unbelievers until Judgement Day are to be shared among all believers. That is, in essence, Moududi's explanation of revelation 59:10, "And it also belongs to those who came after them ... till the Day of Resurrection":

> 59:10 Those who came after them say: "Our Lord, forgive us and our brothers who preceded us in belief and do not instill in our hearts any rancour towards those who believe. Lord, You are indeed Clement and Merciful."

Allah was not impressed with the remaining Jewish tribe of Medina, the Banu Qurayzah, who promised to come to the aid of the Banu Nadir but never showed up. In any event, it would not have made any difference.

> 59:11 Have you not considered the hypocrites? They say to their brethren who have disbelieved from the People of the Book; "If you are driven out, we will go out with you and we will never obey anyone against you; and should anyone fight you, we will certainly support you." Allah bears witness that they are liars, indeed.

> 59:12 If they are driven out, they will not go out with them; and if anyone fights them, they will not support them. Even if they support them, they will turn their backs in flight; then they will not receive any support.

> 59:13 You are indeed more terrifying in their hearts than Allah. That is because they are a people who do not understand.

> 59:14 They do not fight you altogether except in fortified cities or from behind walls. Their prowess is great among

themselves. You think they are united, yet their hearts are at variance. That is because they are a people who do not understand.

59:15 Like those who, shortly before them, tasted the futility of their action. They shall have a painful punishment.

59:16 Like Satan, when he said to man: "Disbelieve"; then, when he disbelieved, he said: "I am quit of you. Indeed, I fear Allah, the Lord of the Worlds."

59:17 Thereupon, their end together was to be in the Fire, dwelling therein forever. That is the reward of the wrongdoer.

With their livelihood gone, the Banu Nadir agreed to go into exile. The Prophet allowed them to take with them whatever their camels could carry. That left the Banu Qurayzah (also referred to as the Beni Qurayzah).

What Allah had to say about the dispossession of the Banu Qaynuqa and the Banu Nadir:

THE MUSTERING

59 Al-Hashr

In the Name of Allah,
the Compassionate, the Merciful

59:1 Everything in the heavens and the earth glorifies Allah. He is the All-Mighty, the All-Wise.

59:2 It is He Who drove out the unbelievers among the People of the Book from their homes at the first mustering. You did not think that they would be driven out, and they thought that their forts would protect them from Allah. Then, Allah seized them from an unexpected quarter and cast terror into their hearts, so that they destroyed their homes with their own hands, as well as the hands of the believers. Reflect, then, O people of perception!

59:3 Had not Allah decreed dispersion upon them, He would certainly have punished them in the present life, and in the Hereafter, the punishment of the Fire shall be theirs.

> 59:4 That is because they have opposed Allah and His Messenger, and he who opposes Allah will find Allah terrible in retribution.

Some of the exiled leaders of the Banu Nadir and Banu Qaynuqa went to Mecca and offered to join the Meccans to fight Muhammad. At first the Meccans were sceptical. To test their allegiance they asked the Jews which was better — paganism or Islam? The Jews answered that paganism was preferable to Muhammad's type of monotheism. The Meccans then accepted the Jews of the Banu Nadir and Banu Qaynuqa as their ally, thereby sealing the fate of the Banu Qurayzah.

Allah was quick to denounce this new unholy alliance of monotheists and polytheists.

> 4:51 Have you not considered those who received a portion of the Book? They believe in idols and demons, and they say to the unbelievers: "Those are more rightly guided than those who believe."
>
> 4:52 Those are the ones whom Allah has cursed; and whomever Allah curses will have no supporter.
>
> 4:53 Or do they have a share in the Kingdom? If so, they will not give the people a speck on a date-stone.
>
> 4:54 Or do they envy the people (the Arabs) for what Allah has given them of His Bounty? For we have given Abraham's family the Book and the Wisdom and bestowed on them a great kingdom.
>
> 4:55 Some of them believed in him, others rejected him. Sufficient is the scourge of Hell.

The Meccans and their allies, including their Jewish allies, which in the Koran are referred to as the Confederates, shortly thereafter marched on Medina with an army numbering an estimated ten thousand men. At this crucial juncture, the leader of the Banu Qurayzah announced his intention not to honour his commitment to come to aid of the Prophet if the Muslims are attacked, and entered into negotiations with the Meccans.

Battle of the Ditch

The battle for Medina is usually referred to as the Battle of the Ditch because of a trench that was dug on the flat approaches to the city[29]. The idea for a trench to counter the superior Meccan cavalry came from a Persian Christian convert to Islam by the name of Salman al Farsi (or Farisi). This *ditch* completely stymied the Meccan forces which included a 300 horse cavalry unit. For two weeks, an army of ten thousand waited for their hapless and befuddled commander Abu Sufyan to devise a strategy to overcome what should have been a minor obstacle.

In the meantime, the go-between in the negotiations for a joint operation between the Meccans and the remaining Jews of Medina against the Muslims, converted to Islam. The quick-thinking Muhammad made Nu'aym ibn Mas'ud his double-agent, asking him to continue acting as go-between and sow distrust between the would-be allies thereby delaying any agreement. It worked. Negotiations were at an impasse when Allah decided to put an end to the siege by sending a vicious sandstorm which wreaked havoc on the exposed Meccan camp which was already short on supplies. He may also have concealed elements of His Air Force (angels, "the host you did no see" in revelation 33:9) in the swirling, grinding sand.

> 33:9 O believers, remember Allah's grace on you when enemy hosts (of confederates allied against Muslims in the Battle of the Ditch (khandaq) during the siege of Medina) came upon you; then We sent against them a wind and hosts you did not actually see. Allah perceives well what you do.

Disconcerted and confused, the Meccans and their allies abandoned the siege of Medina. As at the Battle of Badr, the casualties inflicted by these "hosts" during this desert sitzkrieg were light; casualties for

---

[29] No slaves where employed in the digging of the trench.

Narrated Anas:

Allah's Apostle went towards the Khandaq (i.e. Trench) and saw the Emigrants and the Ansar digging in a very cold morning as they did not have slaves to do that for them.

When he noticed their fatigue and hunger he said, "O Allah! The real life is that of the Here-after, (so please) forgive the Ansar and the Emigrants."

In its reply the Emigrants and the Ansar said, "We are those who have given a pledge of allegiance to Muhammad that we will carry on Jihad as long as we live."

Bukhari 52.87

both sides were 8 Meccans dead and 6 Muslims. However, this is not how Allah saw it:

> 33:10 When they came upon you from above you and from below you, and your eyes looked askew and your hearts reached your throats, while you entertained false thoughts about Allah.
>
> 33:11 Then and there, the believers were sorely tried and shaken very violently.

Verses which may give you an indication of the difficulties faced by the Prophet – the loyalty and commitment of his troops being paramount.

> 33:12 And when the hypocrites and those in whose hearts is a sickness were saying: "Allah and His Messenger have only promised us vanity."
>
> 33:13 And when a group of them said: "O people of Yathrib (Medina), there is no place for you to abide in, so turn back"; while another group of them were seeking the Prophet's permission, saying: "Our homes are exposed", whereas they were not exposed. They only wanted to flee.
>
> 33:14 And were it entered from its different quarters, and then they were asked to apostatize, they would certainly have done so, without lingering but a short while.
>
> 33:15 Although they had made a pledge to Allah, before, that they will not turn their backs. Pledges to Allah are always accountable.
>
> 33:16 Say: "Flight will not profit you, if you flee from death or murder; for then you will not partake of enjoying life except briefly."
>
> 33:17 Say: "Who will defend you against Allah, if He wishes you ill or if He wishes you well." They will find for themselves, apart from Allah, no protectors or supporters.
>
> 33:18 Allah would surely know those of you who hinder the others and those who say to their brothers: "Come over to us"; and they do not partake of fighting, except a little.
>
> 33:19 They are ever niggardly towards you, but if fear overtakes them, you will see them look at you, with their

eyes rolling like one who is in the throes of death. But when fear subsides, they cut you with sharp tongues. They are niggardly in times of prosperity (as a result of the spoils of war); those are no believers. Thus Allah has frustrated their actions, that being for Allah an easy matter.

33:20 They think the Confederates (*the Meccans and their allies*) have not departed, but were the Confederates to show up, they would wish they were desert dwellers with the Bedouins asking about your news. However, were they in your midst, they would fight but little.

33:21 You have had a good example in Allah's Messenger; surely for him who hopes for Allah and the Last Day and remembers Allah often.

33:22 When the believers saw the Confederates, they said: "This is what Allah and His Messenger have promised us, and Allah and His Messenger are truthful." And it only increased them in faith and submission.

33:23 Of the believers, there are men who fulfilled what they pledged to Allah; some of them have died, some are still waiting, without changing in the least.

33:24 So that Allah might reward the truthful for their truthfulness and punish the hypocrites, if He wishes, or forgive them. Surely Allah is All-Forgiving, All-Merciful.

Allah vanquished the Meccans, even if there were no spoils to be had. What a God!

33:25 Allah turned back the unbelievers in a state of rage, having not won any good (spoils), and Allah spared the believers battle. Allah is, indeed, Strong and Mighty.

The Massacre of the Banu Qurayzah

With Medina secure for the time being the Prophet received an order from the angel Gabriel to attack the Banu Qurayzah whose leaders are said to have plotted with the Meccans during the Battle of the Ditch.

> **Narrated Aisha:**
>
> When Allah's Apostle returned on the day (of the battle) of Al-Khandaq (i.e. Trench), he put down his arms and took a bath. Then Gabriel whose head was covered with dust, came to him saying, "You have put down your arms! By Allah, I have not put down my arms yet."
>
> Allah's Apostle said, "Where (to go now)?"
>
> Gabriel said, "This way," pointing towards the tribe of Bani Quraiza. So Allah's Apostle went out towards them.
>
> *Bukhari 52.68*

God's Messenger marched on their fortress just outside Medina with three thousand Jihadists. When he neared the fortress he called out to its defenders: "O brothers of monkeys and pigs! Fear me, fear me."[30]

After twenty five days, the Banu Qurayzah asked for a mediator. The Prophet sent Abu Lubabah who matter-of-factly informed the Jews that the Prophet had slaughter on his mind.

> 'When they saw him (Lubabah), the men rose to meet him, and the women and children rushed to grab hold of him, weeping before him, so that he felt pity for them. They said to him, "Abu Lubabah, do you think that we should submit to Muhammad's judgment"? "Yes", he said, but he pointed with his hand to his throat, that it would be slaughter."'
> *Tabari*

The Banu Qurayzah asked the Prophet to be allowed to go into exile. God's Messenger rejected their proposal and insisted that they submit themselves to his judgement. Abu Lubabah would not be a witness to the result of his negotiations with Jews. It was probably just as well.

> "Abu Lubabah felt guilty that he had broken his promise of secrecy with Muhammad. To atone for his 'misdeed' he

---

[30] In two revelations (2:65 and 7:166) Allah refers to Jews as apes or monkeys; an epithet that may have been meant to apply to future generations (2:66).

2:65 And you surely know those of you who violated the Sabbath; We said to them: "Be [like] dejected apes."

2:66 Thus We made that an example to their contemporaries and to those after them, and an admonition to the righteous.

7:166 Then, when they disdained arrogantly what they were forbidden, We said to them: "Be miserable monkeys."

went straight to the mosque and bound himself with ropes to one of the pillars. This pillar is known as the 'pillar of repentance' or the 'pillars of Abu Lubabah'." *Abul Kasem*

Lubabah spent six days chained to his pillar. He was freed by the Prophet after he received the following revelations in quick succession.

> 8:27 O you who believe, do not betray Allah and the Messenger, nor betray your trust knowingly.

> 9:104 Do they not know that Allah is He who accepts repentance from His servants, and accepts voluntary alms, and that Allah is All-Forgiving, Merciful?

Ignoring Lubabah's warning, the Banu Qurayzah surrendered en-masse to the Prophet. They agreed to a proposal by God's Messenger that a mortally wounded believer by the name of Sad bin Mu'adh decide their fate.

Narrated Abu Said Al-Khudri:

Some people (the Banu Qurayzah) agreed to accept the verdict of Sad bin Mu'adh so the Prophet sent for him.

He came riding a donkey, and when he approached the Mosque, the Prophet said, "Get up for the best amongst you." or said, "Get up for your chief."

Then the Prophet said, "O Sad! These people have agreed to accept your verdict."

Sad said, "I judge that their warriors should be killed and their children and women should be taken as captives."

The Prophet said, "You have given a judgment similar to Allah's Judgment."

Bukhari 58.148

A trench was dug in Medina's marketplace and the estimated seven-hundred male and teenaged boys of the Banu Qurayzah were beheaded with the Prophet of Mercy looking on.

> "...the messenger of God commanded that furrows should be dug in the ground for the B. Qurayzah. Then he sat down, and Ali and al-Zubayr began cutting off their heads in his presence." *Tabari*

'The messenger of God went out into the marketplace of Medina and had trenches dug in it; then he sent for them and had them beheaded in those trenches. They were brought out to him in groups ... They numbered 600 or 700 — the largest estimate says they were between 800 and 900 ... the affair continued until the Messenger of God had finished with them.' *Tabari*

One woman was also beheaded that day. During the siege of the fortress of the Banu Qurayzah she had killed a Muslim soldier by dropping a millstone on his head. Her death as narrated by the Prophet's child bride Aisha.

> Only one of their women was killed. By God, she was by me, talking with me and laughing unrestrainedly while the Messenger of God was killing their men in the marketplace, when suddenly a mysterious voice called out her name, saying, "Where is so and so?"
>
> She said, "I shall be killed."
>
> "Why?" I asked.
>
> She said, "A misdeed that I committed."
>
> She was taken away and beheaded.'
>
> *Aisha*

God's Messenger had ordered that all Jewish males with pubic hair were to be killed, but he did spare one boy who took refuge with a Muslim woman who pleaded with the Prophet to spare the boy's life. Her pleading for mercy may not have been necessary if the following story as told by the boy in question is accurate.

> **Narrated Atiyyah al-Qurazi:**
>
> I was among the captives of Banu Qurayzah. They examined us, and those who had begun to grow hair (pubes) were killed, and those who had not were not killed. I was among those who had not grown hair.
>
> *Abu Dawud 38.4390*

The dead men's wives and daughters were sold into slavery, except for the beautiful widow Rayhanah whom God's Messenger made his concubine. Rayhanah turned down the Prophet's marriage proposal thinking it unseemly considering the recent mass murder of male members of her tribe.

Sad bin Mu'adh also died that day. The Prophet said that Allah's throne shook when he died, so moved was the Almighty by the death of a man who had the courage to cold-bloodily send His enemies to their death and their wives and daughters into slavery.

It should not come as a surprise that Allah was all shook up when he greeted Sad bin Mu'adh in Paradise; after all, not only did He approve of Sad bin Mu'adh's decision, but also of everything that came after: the cold-blooded murder of the men and boys of the Banu Qurayzah, the enslavement of their wives, daughters and sisters and the appropriation of everything they owned by His Messenger?

> 33:26 And He brought those of the People of the Book who supported them from their fortresses and cast terror into their hearts, some of them you slew and some you took captive.
>
> 33:27 And He bequeathed to you their lands, their homes and their possessions, together with land you have never trodden. Allah has power over everything.

News of the massacre spread throughout the Arabian Peninsula and not unlike the massacres committed by those who follow the example of the Prophet today inspired both fear and admiration. One thing the massacre made perfectly clear is that you had to choose a side; you could not remain neutral in the war between the believers and unbelievers of which the Arab civil war was the opening gambit. You either chose to become a Muslim and agreed to fight and kill to establish Allah's Kingdom on earth or you became a target of the believers, to be hunted down and killed.

Many converted to Islam after the massacre, not only because they believed that a man who would do such a thing could not be stopped, but to join in the general pillage of the unbelievers' property. All you had to say was "I declare there is no god except God, and I declare that Muhammad is the Messenger of God" and you could with impunity kill or enslave those who refused to say those magic life-saving words and help yourself to their property, their wives and their daughters for your troubles, and still be guaranteed a place in Paradise.

There is a lesson to be learned in what happened to the Jews of Medina.

Apologist and author of *Muhammad – A Prophet for our Times*, Karen Armstrong writes that the massacre was a tactical necessity, that the Muslims were fighting for their lives. Sending the mothers, wives and daughters of the dead men to join the former Jewish communities of Medina, which the Prophet had sent into exile, would not have had any impact on the tactical or strategic position of the Muslims.

The explanation of Tamam Khan is more to the point, that it was a tradition of the Arabs for the men to share in the plunder, the booty Allah calls it, of those they overpowered in battles or in other venues. The plunder includes the enslavement of the beaten foe, if he is not killed, his sons, wives and daughters.

> After the battle of the Trench [Rayhanah was] marched into the courtyard with the several hundred other women and their children to be claimed as a reward by the Muslim soldiers, while the Qurayzah man were led away to be executed.

Tamam Khan, A History of the Wives of Muhammad

Another of the more primitive Arab traditions that Allah saw fit to establish as a universal unchanging law in his Koran, modified only slightly to exclude the right to the life and property of the believer.

~~~~~~~~~~~~~~~~

> 5:11 O believers, remember Allah's grace upon you, when certain people intended to reach out to you with their hands but Allah restrained them. Fear Allah, and in Allah let the believers put their trust.

Moududi's commentary on what he claims is a reference to an attempt by the Jews of Medina to do away with the Prophet and his companions:

> This alludes to the incident reported by Ibn 'Abbas when a group of Jews invited the Prophet (peace be on him) and a number of his close Companions to dinner. They had in fact hatched a plot to pounce upon the guests and thus undermine the very foundation of Islam. But by the grace of God the Prophet (peace be on him) came to know of the plot at the eleventh hour and did not go.

An Avoidable Tragedy

The Jews of Medina did not blame God for what happened to them, they blamed His Messenger. They worshipped the same monotheistic deity as the Muslims and that god would not have done what the Prophet did to them, revelation 4:78.

> 4:77 Have you not seen those to whom it was said: "Hold back your hands, perform the prayer and give the alms-tax"; but when they were ordered to fight, a group of them appeared to fear men just as they fear Allah, or even more. They said: "Lord, why have you ordered us to fight? If only You would grant us respite for a short period." Say: "The pleasure of this world is small and the Hereafter is far better for the God-fearing; and you will not be wronged a whit."

> 4:78 Wherever you may be, death will overtake you, even if you are in high towers. And if a good fortune befalls them (the Jews) they say: "This is from Allah." But when misfortune befalls them, they say: "It is from you (Muhammad)." Say: "All is from Allah." What is the matter with those people who barely understand any discourse!

> 4:79 Whatever good visits you, it is from Allah; and whatever evil befalls you, it is from yourself; and We have sent you (Muhammad) forth to mankind as a Messenger. Allah is the All-Sufficient Witness!

That the Jews of Medina bear a large responsibility for what happened to them is undeniable. They first welcomed and protected the Prophet Muhammad because they worshipped the same god. They fell out because they could not accept him as a legitimate conduit with the Almighty – that role being reserved for "the chosen people" exclusively.

Muhammad was a Muslim, but also what we would call today an Arab nationalist. The Jews scriptural position meant that the Muslim Arabs would have to accept the equivalent of Jewish suzerainty, a Jewish supremacy that the Torah maintains will eventually encompass all nations.

The Prophet, having borrowed so much from the Torah, borrowed one last communication from the Jewish flavour of their common God: it was the Muslims who were called upon to become rulers of the world because of their claim to the "Superior Religion".

Realizing that they had been outmaneuvered, and not being able to modify their scriptural position to give the Muslims equal billing before God, the Jews of Medina should have all left the city or fought the good fight. They did neither, and the Battle of the Ditch sealed their faith.

The Broken Covenant

> 5:12 Allah made a covenant with the Children of Israel, and We raised among them twelve chieftains. And Allah said: "I am with you. Surely, if you perform the prayer, give the alms, believe in my Messengers and support them and lend Allah a fair loan (spend in the way ordered by Allah), I will forgive you your sins and admit you into Gardens, beneath which rivers flow. But if any one of you disbelieves afterwards, he certainly strays from the right path.

Allah will remind the Jews of Medina, some of whom may have converted to Islam, about this covenant while providing additional specifics meant for them alone.

> 2:83 When We made a covenant with the Children of Israel (saying): "You shall worship none other than Allah; show kindness to your parents, to the near of kin, to the orphans and to the poor; speak to people; perform the prayers, give the alms-tax." But, with the exception of a few, you did not abide by the covenant and you turned away.

> 2:84 And when We made a covenant with you (saying): "You shall not shed your own blood, nor drive your people away from their homes", you accepted and you bore witness [thereto].

> 2:85 Yet there you are killing each other and turning some of your folks from their homes, making common cause against them with sin and aggression. But should they come to you as captives you would ransom them. Surely it was unlawful for you to drive them away. Do you, then, believe in one part (paying the ransom) of the Book and disbelieve in another (killing and driving away their people from their homes)? The reward of those among you who do that is nothing but disgrace in this world, and on the Day of

Resurrection they shall be turned over to the most severe punishment. Allah is not unaware of what you do.

2:86 Those are the people who have traded the life of this world for the Hereafter. Their punishment shall not be lightened, nor shall they be helped.

Sometimes you do have to leave the explanation to the experts. Moududi's commentary on this covenant with the Jews:

> Before the advent of the Prophet (peace be on him) the Jewish tribes who lived on the outskirts of Madina (sic) had concluded an alliance with the Arab tribes of Aws and Khazraj. When the Arab tribes fought against one another each Jewish tribe fought on the side of its allies, which led to fratricide and so to a flagrant violation of the Book of God. Moreover, when the war ended the captives were ransomed. This ransom was justified on the basis of scriptural arguments; they extolled the Word of God when it permitted the ransom of prisoners of war, but attached no significance at all to the same Word of God when it prohibited mutual feuding.

Fakhry, in a footnote, writes that Allah's Covenant included "believing that Muhammad is the Messenger of Allah". The Prophet would, of course, not have been alive when Allah's Covenant with the Jews was first entered into thousands of years earlier, just before He separated them into twelve tribes. This could indicate that the following revelations about a covenant may also have been meant for Jewish contemporaries of God's Messenger.

> 2:40 O Children of Israel, remember the grace which I bestowed on you. Fulfil your covenant (by believing that Muhammad is the Messenger of Allah) and I shall fulfil my Covenant (by rewarding you). And Me alone you should fear.
>
> 2:41 Believe in what I have revealed confirming that which is with you (your Scriptures) and do not be the first to deny it. Do not trade My Revelations for a small price; and Me alone you should fear.
>
> 2:42 And do not confuse truth with falsehood and do not conceal the truth while you know it.

2:43 Perform the prayer; give the alms-tax and bow down with those who bow down.

2:44 Do you command others to be righteous and forget yourselves while you recite the Book? Do you not understand?

2:45 Seek assistance through patience and prayer. It is hard, except for the truly devout;

2:46 Who believe that they shall meet their Lord, and unto Him they shall return.

~~~~~~~~~~~~~~~

What the Jews can look forward to – spending an eternity burning in Hell being a given, as it is for all those with whom Allah is displeased.

62:5 The case of those who were loaded with the Torah, then failed to carry it, is similar to an ass which carries learned books. Wretched is the case of the people who have denounced Allah's Signs. Allah does not guide the wrongdoing people.

62:6 Say: "O you who have adopted Judaism; if you claim to be Allah's friends, apart from other people, then do wish for death, if you are truthful."

62:7 Yet, they will never wish it, due to what their hands have advanced. Allah knows well the wrongdoers.

62:8 Say: "The death from which you flee will surely overtake you. Then you will be turned over to Him Who knows the Unseen and the Seen, and He will inform you about what you used to do."

A Change of Direction - The Qibla Verses

41:37 Of His signs are the night and the day, the sun and the moon. Do not prostrate yourself to the sun or to the moon, but prostrate yourself to Allah Who created them, if it is He you truly worship.

41:38 Should they wax proud (the Meccan pagans), then those with your Lord (the angels, Moududi) do glorify him by night and day, without growing weary.

The first Muslims were required to prostrate themselves in the direction of Jerusalem. It was only after the Prophet's falling out with the Jews of Medina that revelations were received from Allah informing His Messenger about a change of direction. Following are the verses where Allah gives His reasons for this about-face (no pun intended).

> 2:142 The ignorant among the people (among the Jews and polytheist Arabs) will say: "What caused them (the Prophet Muhammad and the believers) to turn away from the former Qibla towards which they used to turn (Jerusalem)?" Say: "To Allah belongs the East and the West. He guides whom He wills towards the Right Path."

> 2:143 And thus We have made you (the Muslim nation) a just nation, so that you may bear witness unto the rest of mankind, and that the Messenger may bear witness unto you. We did not ordain your former Qibla except that We may distinguish those who follow the Messenger from those who turn on their heels (return to disbelief). It was indeed a hard test except for those whom Allah guided. Allah would not allow your faith to be in vain. He is Clement and Merciful to mankind.

> 2:144 Surely, We see your face turned towards heaven (yearning for guidance through revelation). We shall turn you towards a Qibla that will please you. Turn your face then towards the Sacred Mosque (the Sacred Mosque of Mecca, the Ka'ba); and wherever you are turn your faces towards it. Those who were given the Book (the Jews and Christians) certainly know this to be the Truth from their Lord. Allah is not unaware of what they do.

> 2:145 Were you even to come to the People of the Book with every proof, they will not follow your Qibla, nor will you follow their Qibla. Nor will some of them follow the Qibla of the others. And were you to follow their desires after all the knowledge that came to you, surely you would be one of the evil-doers.

> 2:146 Those to whom We gave the Book know him (Muhammad, the Messenger of Allah) as they know their

own sons; but a group of them will knowingly conceal the truth.

2:147 The truth is from your Lord. So do not be one of the doubters.

2:148 To everyone there is a direction towards which he turns. So hasten to do the good works. Wherever you are, Allah will bring you all together (in the Hereafter). Surely Allah has power over all things.

Allah's instructions were not limited to the direction Muslims must face when performing the prayers.

2:149 From whatever place you come out, turn towards the Sacred Mosque. This is indeed the truth from your Lord. Allah is not unaware of what you do.

2:150 From whatever place you come out, turn your faces towards the Sacred Mosque. And wherever you all are, turn your faces towards it, lest people should have cause to argue with you, except for the evil-doers among them. Do not fear them, but fear Me so that I may complete My Grace upon you, and that you be rightly guided.

The Treaty of Hudaibiyah

The victory at Medina did not really solved anything for the Muslims. In fact, it may have left them more vulnerable than before. Many of the Jews the Prophet sent into exile found a new home in the Jewish oasis of Khaybar approximately 153 km to the north of Medina. Khaybar had a pact with Mecca whereby if either city was attacked the other was to march on Medina.

Both city also instituted the equivalent of an economic blockade of Medina. Not only were the Muslim caravans confined to Medina but so were their raiding parties. The believers can no longer depend on plunder to make ends meet. Something has to give. It appears they have no choice. Unless they break the blockade by attacking either Khaybar or Mecca many of the warriors who became Muslims for the booty will leave, or join the Confederates making the fall of Medina and the defeat of the believers inevitable.

The Prophet, to the astonishment of his companions decides to go to Mecca, not to fight, but to perform the lesser pilgrimage, the Umrah. He invites all believers to accompany him on this 800 km round-trip religious trek. The Bedouins among his supporters expect hostilities to break out and do not care to take the war to the holy city of Mecca. They refuse to go. The majority of believers at Medina have no such qualms and look forward to taking the war to the Meccan pagans. They believe the pilgrimage is just a ruse, and that if the Prophet is denied, he will enter Mecca by force.

The men who will accompany God's Messenger are only allowed a sheathed sword as a weapon, and must follow the ritual preparation, much of it borrowed from the pagans, such as fasting, shaving your head and body hair, wearing a simple robe without decorations of any kind and abstaining from sexual relations.

On February 628 the Prophet and an estimated fourteen hundred male pilgrims leave Medina for Mecca where, like the pagans, they hope to circumambulate the Ka'ba while bowing up and down and glorifying their god, the One and only God, Allah.

The Meccans send a small detachment of cavalry to intercept the pilgrims. All are taken prisoners by the Muslims. The Prophet orders that they be released without conditions. The Meccans then send a larger detachment to meet the believers. It arrives only to find the believers prostrated towards Mecca in prayer. Their leader Ikrimah, son of Abu Jahl, will not give the order to attack and simply turns back. God's Messenger then decides to sends an emissary to the Meccans to explain that he has only come to perform the pilgrimage. His envoy and his retinue are intercepted by Ikrimah who cripples they camels and leaves them to make their way back to the Prophet on foot.

Ikrimah and his troops now bar the main route into the sacred perimeter of the holy city. The Prophet avoids a confrontation with Ikrimah by taking an alternate dangerous rocky route among the hills overlooking Mecca. With the holy city spread out before him, his camel refuses to go any further. The Prophet said that an angel barred its way. It is now obvious to God's Messenger that Allah does not want them to go any further.

There is no water where the angel forced them to stop. The Prophet raises his arms towards the heavens and asks Allah for help. A short time later he is joined by a pilgrim who tells the Prophet to dig beneath his feet and he will find water. He does.

God's Messenger wants to send another emissary to the Meccans. His companions would rather they simply march on the city. Uthman, the Prophet's son in law accepts to go and talk to the Meccans. When he is late in returning, rumours start to circulate that he has been killed or is being tortured. The pilgrims are now determined to enter Mecca by force, with or without their Prophet's approval, prompting God's Messenger to demand their unquestioning allegiance at a meeting under one of the few trees. One after the other the believers approach the Prophet and swear absolute obedience. Two revelation about that all-important gathering:

> 48:18 Allah was well-pleased with the believers, when they paid you homage under the tree; so He knew what was in their hearts and sent down the Serenity upon them and rewarded them with a victory near at hand,
>
> 48:19 And with many spoils for them to seize. Allah is All-Mighty, All-Wise.

A short time later, a delegation from Mecca arrives. A ten year non-aggression treaty is signed, the Treaty of Hudaibiyah. Under Hudaibiyah, Muslims will be allowed to perform the pilgrimage the following year and every year during which the treaty is in force.

His followers are very unhappy about having to return to Medina without having performed the pilgrimage, and accuse the Prophet of selling them out. God's Messenger tells them that they have achieved a great victory, and Allah bears him out, adding that He will give them an even greater victory.

THE VICTORY

48 Al-Fath

*In the Name of Allah,
the Compassionate, the Merciful*

48:1 We have indeed given you a manifest victory,

48:2 That Allah may forgive you your former and your later sins, and complete His Blessing upon you and lead you onto a straight path;

48:3 And that Allah may give you a mighty victory.

But that is not enough! Allah will justify not allowing the Muslims to take Mecca by force because of believers among the Meccans. He would of course have given them a bloody victory, revelation 48:12 instead of a paper one, revelation 48:24; but the price if He had led them proceed – the guilt they would have felt if they "unwittingly" killed Meccan believers – was too high, revelation 48:25. If only "they had stood apart" He "would have inflicted on those who disbelieved a painful punishment."

48:22 Had the unbelievers fought you, they would certainly have turned their backs in flight; then they would have found no friend or supporter.

48:23 It is Allah's Way which has gone before; and you will never find any alteration of Allah's Way.

48:24 It is He Who held their hands back from you, and your hands from them in the valley of Mecca, after He gave you victory over them. Allah observed what you do.

48:25 It is they who disbelieved and barred you from the Sacred Mosque, and the offering was prevented from reaching its sacrificial site. Had it not been for some believing men and some believing women, whom you did not know, lest you should trample them and earn thereby the guilt unwittingly, that Allah might thereby admit into His Mercy whomever He wishes. Had they stood apart, We would have inflicted on those of them who disbelieved a painful punishment.

48:26 When the unbelievers instilled in their hearts fierceness, the fierceness of paganism, Allah then sent down His Serenity upon His Messenger and upon the believers, and imposed on them the word of piety, they being more deserving thereof and worthier. Allah has knowledge of everything.

Battle of Khaybar

Narrated Anas:

The Prophet set out for Khaibar and reached it at night. He used not to attack if he reached the people at night, till the day broke. So, when the day dawned, the Jews came out with their bags and spades. When they saw the Prophet; they said, "Muhammad and his army!"

The Prophet said, "Allahu Akbar! (Allah is Greater) and Khaibar is ruined, for whenever we approach a nation (i.e. enemy to fight) then it will be a miserable morning for those who have been warned."

Bukhari 52.195

That mighty victory would come only two years into the ten year non-aggression pact. The Prophet will use the breathing space provided by the *Treaty of Hudaibiyah* to complete the encirclement of Mecca. In the meantime, he will deliver the spoils promised by Allah in revelation 48:19 by attacking Khaybar. Under the Treaty of Hudaibiyah, Mecca must remain neutral *in disputes between the Muslims and their enemies.*

The eight "fortresses" of Khaybar fall to the Muslims in just ten days. Apart from a tribute of gold, silver and confiscation of arms, the Jews are allowed to continue to farm the oasis of Khaybar with half of whatever they produce going to the believers. A revelation about the conquest of Khaybar:

> 48:20 Allah has promised you many spoils, for you to take, and He has hastened this one (the spoils of Khaybar) and held the hands of people back of you (*the clause in the Treaty of Hudaibiyah that prevented the Meccans from intervening*), that it may be a sign to the believers and that He might guide you to the straight path.

The Bedouins who refused to accompany the Prophet on his attempted pilgrimage to Mecca, were denied Khaybar. But the Prophet, always thinking ahead, will give them a chance to redeem themselves, revelation 48:16, in what he expects will be a much bigger challenge, the taking of Mecca.

> 48:11 The Bedouins who stayed behind will say to you: "Our possessions and our families preoccupied us; so ask forgiveness for us." They say with their tongues what is not in their hearts. Say: "Who can avail you anything against Allah, if He wishes to harm you or He wishes to profit you? No, Allah is fully aware of what you do.

> 48:12 "Rather, you thought that the Messenger and the believers will never return to their families; and that was embellished in your hearts and you entertained evil thoughts and were a useless people."

> 48:13 He who does not believe in Allah and His Messenger, We have, indeed, prepared for the unbelievers a blazing fire.

> 48:14 To Allah belongs the dominion of the heavens and the earth; He forgives whomever He wishes and punishes whomever He wishes. Allah is All-Forgiving and Merciful.

> 48:15 Those who stayed behind will say, when you set out after certain spoils to seize them: "Let us follow you"; intending to change Allah's Words. Say: "You shall not follow us; thus has Allah said already." They will then say: "No, you are jealous of us." Rather, they understand but a little.

> 48:16 Say to those who stayed behind: "You shall be called up against a people of great might; you shall fight them or they shall submit. If, then, you obey, He will grant you a fair wage; but if you turn away as you turned away before, He will inflict a painful punishment upon you."

Some who did not make the journey were not to blame:

> 48:17 The blind are not to blame, nor the cripple is to blame, nor the sick are to blame. Whoever obeys Allah and His Messenger, He will admit him into Gardens beneath which

rivers flow; but he who turns away, He will inflict upon him a painful punishment.

~~~~~~~~~~~~~

There is more to being a believer than simply saying "we submit" as the Bedouins have yet to discover.

> 49:14 The Bedouins say: "We believe." Say: "You do not believe, but say: 'We submit'; for belief has not yet entered your hearts. If you obey Allah and His Messenger, He will not stint you any of your works. Allah is surely All-Forgiving and Merciful."

> 49:15 Indeed, the believers are those who have believed in Allah and His Messenger, then were not in doubt, but struggle with their possessions and themselves in the Cause of Allah. Those are the truthful ones.

> 49:16 Say: "Will you inform Allah about your religion, while Allah knows what is in the heavens and in the earth? Allah has knowledge of everything."

> 49:17 They regard it a favour to you that they have submitted. Say: "Do not regard your submission a favour to me; rather Allah has favoured you when He guided you to belief, if you are really truthful.

> 49:18 "Allah knows the secrets of the heavens and the earth, and Allah sees well the things you do."

Mecca Surrenders

In January 630, on the pretence that the Meccans have been supplying arms to the Banu Bakr, a tribe allied with the Meccans which has been fighting a tribe allied with the Muslims, the Banu Khuzah, (the Meccans deny this and offer to compensate the Muslims for any damage the Banu Bakr may have caused, to no avail) the Prophet, at the head of an army numbering at least ten thousand, marches on Mecca which is now surrounded by tribes who have converted to Islam or are allies of the Muslims.

Except for a small skirmish, the Meccans, on the advice of their commander Abu Sufyan who tells them that the situation is hopeless, surrender en masse and agree to become Muslim, but not before obtaining a concession from the Prophet, which he will repudiate the next day after he has complete control of Mecca, that they may continue worshipping the goddesses al-Lat, al-Uzza and Manat, the so-called *Satanic Verses*.

After the surrender of Mecca, God's Messenger discretely ordered the murder of six defenceless men and four defenceless women, while pardoning the well-armed, for which he earned the moniker Prophet of Mercy.

Narrated Anas bin Malik:

Allah's Apostle entered Mecca in the year of its Conquest wearing an Arabian helmet on his head and when the Prophet took it off, a person came and said, "Ibn Khatal is holding the covering of the Ka'ba (taking refuge in the Ka'ba)."

The Prophet said, "Kill him."

Bukhari 29.72

Khatal was one of the Prophet's Zakat (charity) collectors who later abandon Islam and returned to Mecca. Khatal sought the protection of the Ka'ba to no avail. Two of the four women put to death were singers in Khatal's household who years earlier as girls had sang satirical songs about God's Messenger. This may, in part, explain the Prophet's pathological aversion to women singers.

Two differing hadiths as to what the Prophet did after the murder of Khatal was taken care of.

Narrated Abdullah:

When the Prophet entered Mecca on the day of the Conquest, there were 360 idols around the Ka'ba. The Prophet started striking them with a stick he had in his hand and was saying, "Truth has come and Falsehood will neither start nor will it reappear.

Bukhari 59.583

Narrated Ibn Abbas:

When Allah's Apostle arrived in Mecca, he refused to enter the Ka'ba while there were idols in it. So he ordered that they be taken out.

The pictures of the (Prophets) Abraham and Ishmael, holding arrows of divination in their hands, were carried out.

The Prophet said, "May Allah ruin them (i.e. the infidels) for they knew very well that they (i.e. Abraham and Ishmael) never drew lots by these (divination arrows).

Then the Prophet entered the Ka'ba and said. "Allahu Akbar" in all its directions and came out and not offered any prayer therein.

Bukhari 59.584

After the surrender, Allah did not object to the believers making friends with the Meccan unbelievers, most of whom were their kin who would shortly be compelled to convert to Islam.

60:7 It may be that Allah will establish friendship between you and those of them who were your enemies. Allah is All-Powerful, and Allah is All-Forgiving, All-Merciful.

60:8 Allah does not forbid you, regarding those who did not fight you and did not drive you out of your homes, to be generous to them and deal with them justly. Allah surely loves the just.

60:9 Allah only forbids you, regarding those who fought you in religion and drove you out of your homes and assisted in driving you out, to take them for friends. Those who take them for friends are, indeed, the wrongdoers.

A verse celebrating the fall of Mecca from the appropriately titled surah, *The Victory*.

48:27 Allah has fulfilled His Messenger's vision in truth: "You shall enter the Sacred Mosque, if Allah wishes, in security, your heads shaved and your hair cut short, without fear." For He knew what you did not know and gave you prior to that, victory near at hand (Khaybar).

Not long after the Meccan surrender, the Prophet will call upon all inhabitants of the Peninsula to become Muslims within four months or face death or enslavement at the hands of the believers. It does not matter that they have never wished or done any harm to the Muslims.

With the Meccans on board, the Prophet liquidated the remaining opposition to Islamic rule on the Peninsula beginning with a large force that was descending on the newly surrendered city.

Spend Freely and Spend Wisely

The conquest of Mecca is only the beginning, as is evident in Allah's demand that the believers "spend freely" of what He "has bequeathed", revelation 57:7; and wisely, revelation 57:10.

57:7 Believe in Allah and His Messenger and spend freely from what He has bequeathed to you. For those of you who believe and spend freely will have a great wage.

57:8 What is the matter with you? You do not believe in Allah, although the Messenger calls upon you to believe in your Lord, and He has already taken your covenant, if you are true believers?

57:9 It is He Who sends down upon His servant manifest Signs, so as to bring you out from the dark shadows into the light. Allah is indeed All-Clement and Merciful towards you.

57:10 And why is it that you do not spend freely in the Cause of Allah, when to Allah belongs the heritage of the heavens and the earth? Not all those of you who spent freely before the Conquest (of Mecca) and have fought are equal. However they are higher in rank than those who spend freely and fought afterwards; and unto each Allah has promised the fairest reward. Allah is Fully Aware of what you do.

57:11 Who is he that will lend Allah a fair loan, that He might double it for him; and he will have a generous wage.

Battle of Hunayn

Muhammad had entered Mecca as both a pilgrim and a conqueror only two weeks earlier when he received reports of an army of unbelievers marching on the city. The Prophet quickly assembled a force of twelve thousand warriors, which included a large detachment of Meccans estimated at two thousand. For the first time the Muslim army largely outnumbered the unbelievers which consisted of warriors from four tribes: the Thaqif, Hawazin, Sa'd and Jasam. The believers almost lost the Battle of Hunayn (also spelled Hunain), when upon entering a narrow passage into the valley of Hunayn, situated between Mecca and Ta'if, they were met by a shower of arrows and fled in disarray.

God's Messenger stood his ground[31] and with the help of Ibn Abbas, the man with the booming voice who shouted the Prophet's words, reminded the believers of their duty to him and to God. The fleeing believers returned to the battle, and their superior numbers and new-found determination won the day, or so it seemed.

Allah reminded the victors, like at the Battle of Badr, that the victory was His for it was He who got His Messenger and the believers to calm down and return to the fight. And like at the Battle of Badr, He sent down invisible warriors, assumed to be angels, to hold back the unbelievers while the Muslims steeled themselves for a successful counterattack.

---

[31] **Narrated Abu Ishaq**:

Somebody asked Al-Bar-a bin 'Azib, "Did you flee deserting Allah's Apostle during the battle of Hunain?"

Al-Bara replied, "But Allah's Apostle did not flee. The people of the Tribe of Hawazin were good archers. When we met them, we attacked them, and they fled. When the Muslims started collecting the war booty, the pagans faced us with arrows, but Allah's Apostle did not flee. No doubt, I saw him on his white mule and Abu Sufyan was holding its reins and the Prophet was saying, 'I am the Prophet in truth: I am the son of 'Abdul Muttalib.' " *Bukhari 52.116*

9:25 Allah gave you victory in numerous places and on the day of Hunayn (a valley between Mecca and Ta'if) when you were pleased with your large number; but it availed you nothing and the land became too straight for you, despite its breath, whereupon you turned back and fled.

9:26 Then Allah sent down His Tranquility upon His Messenger and upon the believers, and He sent down soldiers you did not see, and punished the unbelievers. That is the reward of the unbelievers.

The Muslims followed the retreating unbelievers to their Hawazin fortress city of Ta'if about 75 miles from Mecca and laid siege to the town. After about a month, the defenders sent emissaries to the Prophet to ask for peace and to beg for mercy, and it was granted.

9:27 Then, Allah will pardon thereafter whom He pleases. Allah is All-Forgiving, Merciful.

However, there was no question of returning the booty which some have estimated at six thousand captives, including women and children, forty thousand sheep and goats, four thousand ounces of silver and twenty four thousand camels. The allocation of the booty led to the usual disagreements, in this instance, it was about the Meccans getting a greater share than those who had been fighting with the Prophet since the beginning[32].

The Prophet was using the booty to strengthen the allegiance of the Meccans. As to the complainers, he rebuffed their accusations, in part, by reminding them that: "Were you not poor and God through

---

[32] **Narrated Abu Qatada:**

Allah's Apostle said on the Day of (the battle of) Hunain, "Whoever has killed an infidel and has a proof or a witness for it, then the salb (arms and belongings of that deceased) will be for him."

I stood up to seek a witness to testify that I had killed an infidel but I could not find any witness and then sat down. Then I thought that I should mention the case to Allah's Apostle (and when I did so) a man from those who were sitting with him said, "The arms of the killed person he has mentioned, are with me, so please satisfy him on my behalf."

Abu Bakr said, "No, he will not give the arms to a bird of Quraish and deprive one of Allah's lions of it who fights for the cause of Allah and His Apostle."

Allah's Apostle stood up and gave it to me, and I bought a garden with its price, and that was my first property which I owned through the war booty ...

Bukhari 89.282

me made you rich?" To which they replied: "Verily, God and His Prophet have been kind to us."

They would get even richer as the campaign to rid the Peninsula, and eventually the known world of unbelievers took on a new urgency.

EXPANSION

Announcing a Universal War

Narrated Abu Huraira:

Allah's Apostle said, "I have been ordered to fight with the people till they say, 'None has the right to be worshipped but Allah,' and whoever says, 'None has the right to be worshipped but Allah,' his life and property will be saved by me except for Islamic law, and his accounts will be with Allah, (either to punish him or to forgive him.)"

Bukhari 52.196

41:53 We shall show them Our Signs in the distant regions and in their own souls, until it becomes clear to them that it is the Truth. Does it not suffice your Lord that He is a Witness of Everything?

41:54 Lo and behold, they are in doubt regarding the encounter of their Lord. Lo, He truly encompasses everything.

Istanbul's Topkapi Palace, which is now a museum, was home to all the Ottoman sultans until the reign of Abdulmecid I (1839-1860), a period of nearly four centuries. In the Holy Treasury within the third courtyard of the old palace there is a letter. The more than a thousand-year-old letter, now a shrunken piece of parchment, is carefully preserved behind glass. It is one of the letters that the Prophet Muhammad sent to the various rulers of the kingdoms that bordered Arabia at the time of the Muslim conquest of the peninsula, inviting them, and their subjects, to become Muslims.

The Prophet's ultimatum to his neighbours to convert or Islam will be imposed by force followed a less formal warning to the remaining tribes of Arabia shortly after the surrender of Mecca. His fellow Arabs had four months to convert to Islam after which they stood outside the law – Koranic law – and could be robbed, killed or enslaved by any Muslim.

The letter under glass in the old Topkapi Palace in Istanbul is addressed to the governor of Egypt, a fellow by the name of Muqawqis. The last sentence of the letter God's Messenger sent to Muqawqis has a particularly ominous tone (*italics* mine).

> From Muhammad the servant and Prophet of Allah, to Muqawqis, the leader of the Coptic tribe. There is safety and security for those believers who follow the correct path. Therefore I invite you to accept Islam. If you accept it, you shall find security, save your throne, and gain twice as much reward for having introduced Islam to your followers. If you refuse this invitation, let the sin of calamity which awaits your followers be upon you. You too are People of the Book; therefore let us come to a word common between us that we worship none but Allah and shall equalise anything with him. Let us not abandon Allah and take others for lords other than him. *If you do not consent to this invitation, bear witness that we are Muslims.*

If you do not consent, *we are Muslims;* we do not make idle threats. A warning Allah echoes in a revelation.

> 3:64 Say: "O People of the Book, come to an equitable word between you and us, that we worship none but Allah, do not associate anything with Him and do not set each other as lords besides Allah." If they turn their backs, say: "Bear witness that we are Muslims."

In the letter, the phrase "and gain twice as much reward for having introduced Islam to your followers" is a reminder that Jihad is very much about plunder, for the additional riches can only come from those who refuse Islam, refuse to Submit, and therefore can legally be dispossessed of all they own, then killed or enslaved along with their wives and children.

The intimidating letters did not have the desired effect and the Prophet and his successors made good on the threat they contained. Within twenty short years after the Prophet's death, Muslim armies, during the period known as the Rashidun (the reign of the first four successors to the Prophet known as the Rightly Guided Caliphs), imposed Muslim rule on Persia (including modern day Iraq), Syria, Armenia, Egypt and most of North Africa.

This letter makes a mockery of the claim by apologists, such as Karen Armstrong, that the war of expansion which immediately followed the conquest of the Arab peninsula by the Muslims, was a defensive war.

Muqawqis "ordered that the letter should be placed in an ivory casket, to be kept safely in the government treasury", an important first precaution in ensuring its preservation.

It is mostly to Islamic scholars and historians to whom we are indebted for reporting on what Muqawqis said and did in response to the Prophet's invitation and which includes the following letter:

> From Muqawqis I read your letter and understood what you have written. I know that the coming of a Prophet is still due. But I thought, he would be born in Syria – I have treated your messenger with respect and honor. I am sending two maids (Maria al-Qibtiyya and her sister Sirin) for you as presents. These maids belong to a very respectable family amongst us. In addition I send for you clothes and a Duldul (steed) for riding. May God bestow security on you[33].

Muqawqis' response would indicate that he both respected and perhaps feared God's Messenger (the reason for the tribute of fine Egyptian fabrics, a stallion[34] and the two slave-girls/sisters[35]) and that he knew what would please God's Messenger.

It was this same Muqawqis, also known as Cyrus, Patriarch of Alexandria, who negotiated a separate peace with the Muslims on behalf of the Coptic Christians, which included

---

[33] According to scholar Ibn Sa'd [784-845] the Prophet said, upon receiving the letter and the tribute: "Miserable man! He would not risk his sovereignty but the sovereignty he loves so much will not remain!"

[34] Scholars such as Ibn Sayyid [1944-2004] argue that it was a white mule and a donkey, and that the tribute included gold, a crystal glass and perfumes.

[35] Some have disputed Islam's account of what Muqawqis said and did after receiving the Prophet's ultimatum. The two main sticking point appear to be 1) "Why would a Christian bishop send two Christian ladies, belonging to noble Coptic families, as slaves to a non-Christian ruler?" and 2) "Christian believe in the Second Coming, not in the arrival of a new prophet i.e. the Prophet Muhammad." One explanation is that Muqawqis was a secret convert to Islam and that would explain what he said and did, including facilitating the Muslim conquest of Egypt.

agreeing to pay the jizya[36], when the believers invaded Egypt about ten years after the ultimatum was received. This early capitulation allowed a relatively small Arab invasion force (later re-enforced by desert bedouins when it became evident that Egypt was ripe for the taking and plunder was to be had, followed by veterans of the northern campaigns to gain converts to Islam e.g. Syria) to quickly take complete control of what was then a key province of the Byzantine Empire.

Muqawqis, when the Byzantines repudiated his treaty with the Muslims, is said to have asked their commander, Amr ibn al-As, to "not make peace with them, but treat them as captives and slaves" meaning that the life-saving jizya would not be available to the vanquished.

God's Messenger followed up his declaration of a universal war with a military expedition against Byzantium. It may have been one of the nineteen alluded to in the following hadith:

Narrated Abu Ishaq:

Once, while I was sitting beside Zaid bin Al-Arqam, he was asked, "How many Ghazwat (military expedition) did the Prophet undertake?"

Zaid replied, "Nineteen."

Bukhari 59.285

It would be left up to the Prophet's second successor, Caliph Umar, to successfully invade the old Kingdom and capture Jerusalem.

> Umar sent the Muslims to the great countries to fight the pagans.
>
> When Al-Hurmuzan (a Persian noble) embraced Islam, Umar said to him. "I would like to consult you regarding these countries which I intend to invade."
>
> Al-Hurmuzan said, "Yes, the example of these countries and their inhabitants who are the enemies of the Muslims, is like a bird with a head, two wings and two legs; If one of its wings got broken, it would get up over its two legs, with one wing and the head; and if the other wing got broken, it would get up with

---

[36] People of the Book e.g. Christians and Jews are not to be killed if they refuse to become Muslims, if they are submissive and agree to pay a poll-tax (a tax levied on people rather than on property) called jizya so that their lives might be spared.

two legs and a head, but if its head got destroyed, then the two legs, two wings and the head would become useless.

The head stands for Khosrau[37], and one wing stands for Caesar and the other wing stands for Faris. So, order the Muslims to go towards Khosrau."

So, Umar sent us (to Khosrau) appointing An-Numan bin Muqrin as our commander. When we reached the land of the enemy, the representative of Khosrau came out with forty-thousand warriors, and an interpreter got up saying, "Let one of you talk to me!"

Al-Mughira replied, "Ask whatever you wish."

The other asked, "Who are you?"

Al-Mughira replied, "We are some people from the Arabs; we led a hard, miserable, disastrous life: we used to suck the hides and the date stones from hunger; we used to wear clothes made up of fur of camels and hair of goats, and to worship trees and stones. While we were in this state, the Lord of the Heavens and the Earths, Elevated is His Remembrance and Majestic is His Highness, sent to us from among ourselves a Prophet whose father and mother are known to us.

Our Prophet, the Messenger of our Lord, has ordered us to fight you till you worship Allah Alone or give Jizya (i.e. tribute); and our Prophet has informed us that our Lord says: "Whoever amongst us is killed (i.e. martyred), shall go to Paradise to lead such a luxurious life as he has never seen, and whoever amongst us remain alive, shall become your master."
...

Bukhari 53.386

---

[37] Khosrau II was the last great king of the Sasanian Empire, 590 to 628. The Sasanian was the last Persian Empire (224 AD to 651 AD) before the Muslim conquest. Khosrau would have been dead for a number of years when this conversation is alleged to have taken place, but not perhaps "Caesar" a reference to Heraclius, the Byzantine Emperor from 610 to 641.

To be relegated to mere servants of the practitioners of the superior religion may be the fate reserved for all unbelievers, the Prophet's predictions about the course of the war to establish Allah's Kingdom on earth having proven, in many instances, remarkably accurate.

Narrated Jabir bin Samura:

The Prophet said, "When Khosrau perishes (the last great king of the Sasanian Empire, 590 to 628), there will be no more Khosrau after him, and when Caesar perishes, there will be no more Caesar after him,"

The Prophet also said, "You will spend the treasures of both of them in Allah's Cause."

Bukhari 56.816

Tabuk

The Prophet gave credence to his plans to take his battle to the unbelievers far and wide with an expedition to Tabuk in northwestern Saudi Arabia, then part of the Byzantine Empire. He assembled an army of more than 30 thousand and marched north 889 kms (552 miles) intending to engage the Byzantine forces at Tabuk. The Byzantine did not show up. The lesson was not lost on the locals, not only Arabs but many Christians who flocked to the Prophet's banner. When the Muslims returned there would be no stopping them.

The expedition to Tabuk was one battle too far for many of the believers. They asked to stay behind and, to Allah's initial dismay, His Messenger agreed.

> 9:38 O Believers, what is the matter with you? If you are told: "March forth in the Way of Allah", you simply cling heavily to the ground. Are you satisfied with the present life rather than the Hereafter? Yet the pleasures of the present life are very small compared with those of the Hereafter.
>
> 9:39 If you do not march forth, He will inflict a very painful punishment on you and replace you by another people, and you will not harm him (the Prophet) in the least; for Allah has power over everything.
>
> 9:40 If you do not support him, Allah did support him, when the unbelievers drove him out – he being the second of two (the Prophet and Abu Bakr), while they were both in the cave[38]. He said to his companion: "Do not grieve; Allah is with us." Whereupon, Allah sent down His Tranquility

---

[38] This is another occasion when Allah sent invisible soldiers to guard the entrance to a cave in Thaur mountain where God's Messenger and Abu Bakr were hiding on their way to Medina from Mecca where the Prophet had escaped another assignation attempt.

upon him and assisted him with soldiers you did not see, and made the word of the unbelievers the lowest. The Word of Allah is indeed the highest and Allah is Mighty and Wise.

9:41 Charge forth, on foot or mounted, and struggle with your possessions and yourselves in the Way of Allah. That is far better for you, if only you knew.

9:42 Had it been a gain near at hand and a short journey, they would surely have followed you. But the distance seemed too long to them. Still they will swear by Allah: "Had we been able, we would have marched forth with you." They damn themselves, and Allah knows that they are liars.

Allah had choice words for His Messenger and questioned the allegiance of many of those who sought to avoid the long journey north.

9:43 May Allah pardon you! Why did you allow them (to stay behind) before it became clear to you who were the truthful ones, and you knew who were the liars?

9:44 Those who believe in Allah and the Last Day do not ask you for [exemption from] fighting in the Way of Allah with their wealth and lives. Allah knows well the righteous.

9:45 Only those who do not believe in Allah and the Last Day will ask you [for exemption] and their hearts are in doubt. Thus they vacillate in their state of doubt.

Allah then changes His tune, as He often does in these situations, and explains that it was all His doing if some of them were reluctant to join the Prophet on his expedition to the southern frontier of the Byzantine Empire.

9:46 Had they wanted to go forth, they would have made preparations for that; but Allah was averse to their going forth, and so He held them back, and it was said to them: "Sit back with those who sit back."

9:47 Had they gone out with you, they would have only increased your confusion, and would have kept moving among you sowing sedition. And some of you would have listened to them. Allah knows well the wrongdoers.

> 9:48 They have sought to sow sedition before and turned things around for you, until the truth came out and Allah's Command was manifested, although they were averse [to it].
>
> 9:49 Some of them say: "Allow me and do not tempt me." Indeed they have already fallen into temptation and Hell shall encompass the unbelievers.
>
> 9:50 If a good fortune befalls you, they are displeased, and if a disaster befalls you they say: "We took our precautions before." Then, they turn away rejoicing.
>
> 9:51 Say: "Nothing will befall us except what Allah has decreed for us. He is our Lord, and in Allah let the believers put their trust."

Allah tells His Messenger to remind those who wish to stay behind that he, the Prophet, is also His instrument for meting out punishment.

> 9:52 Say: "Do you expect for us anything other than one of the two fairest outcome (martyrdom or victory); while we await for you that Allah will smite you with a punishment, either from Himself, or at our hands?" So wait and watch, we are waiting and watching with you.

Some wanted to offer money to get an exemption from this Jihad against the Byzantines.

> 9:53 Say: "Spend willingly or unwillingly; it shall not be accepted from you. You are truly a sinful people."
>
> 9:54 And nothing prevents what they spend from being accepted but that they disbelieve in Allah and His Messenger and that they do not perform the prayer except lazily, and do not spend [anything] except grudgingly.

The Prophet may have granted exemptions to fathers who did not want to be away from their children for months on end. This did not sit well with Allah, Who explained that even children were part of His Plan, therefore not a valid reason to be exempted from the fighting, no matter how far.

> 9:55 So do not let their wealth and their children win your approval, Allah only wishes to torture them therewith in

the present life, so that their souls might depart while they are still unbelievers.

Why some did not care to accompany God's Messenger on a long journey:

> 9:56 They swear by Allah that they [are believers] like you, but they are not; they are a people who [fear] you.
>
> 9:57 If they could find a shelter or dens or any place to crawl into, they would make for it in great haste.

It was during the return trip from Tabuk that the Prophet got wind of an alleged assassination plot which led to some foreboding revelations about unbelievers and hypocrites.

> 9:73 O Prophet, fight the unbelievers and the hypocrites and be stern with them. Their abode is Hell, and what a terrible fate!
>
> 9:74 They swear by Allah that they said nothing [evil], but they said the word of disbelief and disbelieved after professing Islam, and they aimed at (according to some commentators they aimed at killing the Prophet while he was returning from Tabuk) what they could not attain. They only resented that Allah and His Messenger have enriched them from His Bounty. If they repent, it will be better for them; but if they turn away, Allah will inflict a very painful punishment on them in this world and the Hereafter, and they will have on earth no friend or supporter.
>
> 9:75 And some of them make a compact with Allah: "If He give us of His Bounty, we shall give in charity and be among the righteous."
>
> 9:76 But when He gave them of His Bounty, they grew mean and turned away disobediently.
>
> 9:77 So He caused hypocrisy to cling to their hearts until the day they meet Him, on account of revoking what they promised Allah and on account of lying.
>
> 9:78 Do they not know that Allah knows their hidden thoughts and private talk, and that Allah knows fully the things unseen?

> 9:79 Those disparage the believers who give voluntary alms and those find nothing to offer but their outmost endeavour, and they scoff at them. May Allah mock them. There is a painful punishment [in store] for them.
>
> 9:80 Ask forgiveness for them or do not ask forgiveness for them. If you ask forgiveness for them seventy times, Allah will not forgive them; because they disbelieve in Allah and His Messenger. Allah does not guide the sinful people.

Some may have stayed behind because they were worried about the heat.

> 9:81 Those who stayed behind rejoiced at tarrying behind the Messenger of Allah and hated to struggle with their wealth and their lives in Allah's Path, saying: "Do not march forth in the heat." Say: "The Fire of Hell is hotter, if only they could understand."
>
> 9:82 Let them laugh a little and cry a lot, as a reward for what they used to do.

While Allah waited to burn those who stayed behind in Hell, His Messenger was not allowed to have them join him on further expeditions.

> 9:83 Then, if Allah brings you back to a party of them and they ask your permission to go forth with you, say: "You will never go forth with me, and you will never fight with me against any enemy. You were content to sit back the first time; so sit back with those who stay behind."

As to attending their funeral, don't bother:

> 9:84 And do not ever pray over any one of them who dies, or be present at their grave; indeed they disbelieve in Allah and His Messenger, and died still ungodly

Again with the children and the wealthy!

> 9:85 And do not let their wealth or children win your admiration. Allah only wishes to punish them therewith in the present life, so that their souls may depart while they are still unbelievers.

Perhaps the ultimate insult, revelation 9:87.

> 9:86 And if a Surah is revealed stating: "Believe in Allah and fight along with His Messenger", the affluent among them will ask your permission and say: "Let us be with those who stay behind."
>
> 9:87 They are content to be among the women who stay behind, and a seal is set upon their hearts, and thus they do not understand.

What those who went to Tabuk can expect:

> 9:88 But the Messenger and those who believe with him struggle with their wealth and their lives. To those are the good things reserved, and those are the prosperous.
>
> 9:89 Allah has prepared for them Gardens beneath which rivers flow, abiding therein forever. That is the great triumph!

Even the desert Arabs i.e. bedouins don't escape Allah's criticism.

> 9:90 Some of the desert Arabs who gave excuses came to seek permission, whereas those who lied to Allah and His Messenger stayed behind. Those of them who disbelieved shall be afflicted with a very painful punishment.

Allah did allow for some exceptions for the weak and the sick and for those who could not afford to make the journey to Tabuk, and those for whom transportation was not available.

> 9:91 The weak, the sick, and those who have nothing to spend are not at fault, if they are true to Allah and His Messenger. There can be no blame on the beneficent; and Allah is All-Forgiving, Merciful.
>
> 9:92 Nor on those who, when they came to you asking you for mounts, you said: "I do not find that whereon I can mount you." Thereupon they went back, their eyes overflowing with tears, sorrowing for not finding the means to spend (to provide the expenses of war).

As often happens during these long rants, Allah repeats himself, perhaps for effect.

> 9:93 The blame is on those who ask your permission,

> although they are rich. They are content to join those women who stay behind. Allah has placed a seal upon their hearts and so they do not know.

More revelations, supposedly received on the return journey, about the people the Prophet allowed to stay behind, prompting another round of questioning when God's Messenger reached Medina.

> 9:94 They present to you [false] excuses when you return to them. Say: "Do not offer excuses; we will not believe you. Allah has told us [all] about you. Allah shall see your work, and His Messenger too. Then you will be turned over to Him Who knows the unseen and the seen, and He will apprise you of what you used to do."
>
> 9:95 They will swear by Allah to you, when you return to them, that you may leave them alone. So leave them alone; they are an abomination and their abode is Hell, as a reward for what they used to do.
>
> 9:96 They swear to you that you may be well-pleased with them; but should you be well-pleased with them, Allah will not be well-pleased with the sinful people.

Generalizations about Bedouins:

> 9:97 The desert Arabs are more steeped in unbelief and hypocrisy and are more likely not to know the bounds of what Allah has revealed to His Messenger. Allah is All-Knowing, Wise.
>
> 9:98 And some of the desert Arabs regard what they spend as a fine, and await the turns of fortune to go against you. May the evil turn against them. Allah is All-Hearing, All-Knowing.
>
> 9:99 And some of the desert Arabs believe in Allah and the Last Day and regard what they spend [in the way of Allah] as a means to get closer to Allah and to earn the prayers of the Messenger. Indeed, that will bring them closer [to Allah]. He will admit them into His Mercy. Allah is truly All-Forgiving, Merciful.

Some of the desert Arabs and some of the people of Medina can expect double the punishment.

> 9:101 And some of the desert Arabs around you are hypocrites, and some of the people of Medina persist in hypocrisy. You do not know them, but We know them. We shall punish them twice, then they will be afflicted with a terrible punishment (before they are thrown into the Fire).

Some confessed that they had lied to avoid going to Tabuk. Allah hints that He will pardon them if they part with some of their wealth. There may also have been some labour involved, revelation 9:105.

> 9:102 Others have confessed their sins; they mixed a good deed with a bad one (the good deed is confessing sins and the bad one is that they stayed behind when the Muslims marched against the enemy). Perhaps Allah will pardon them. Allah is truly All-Forgiving, Merciful.
>
> 9:103 Take of their wealth voluntary alms to purify and cleanse them therewith; and pray for them, for your prayers are a source of tranquility for them. Allah is All-Hearing, All-Knowing.
>
> 9:104 Do they not know that Allah is He who accepts the repentance from His servants, and accepts voluntary alms, and that Allah is All-Forgiving, Merciful?
>
> 9:105 And say: "Work, for Allah shall see your work, and His Messenger and the believers too. And you shall be brought back (on the Day of Resurrection) to Him Who knows the unseen and the seen, and He will apprise you of what you used to do."

As to any others We have not revealed anything about, I will decide when the Day comes.

> 9:106 And others are deferred to Allah's Decree; He will either punish them or pardon them. And Allah is All-Knowing, Wise.

The Destruction of the Christian Mosque of Medina

It was also on the way back from Tabuk that Allah revealed what He thought about the mosque built by the Christian monk Abu 'Amir al Rahib, and those who prayed there. The Masjid al-Dirar had been built, with the Prophet's approval, next to the Masjid al-Quba whose first stones were positioned by the Prophet himself. After receiving the revelation that He should not pray there, God's Messenger realized that it had been a mistake to allow its construction and had the Masjid al-Dirar destroyed.

The fact that the Christian mosque was built with the Prophet's approval would indicate that Abu 'Amir's intentions were honourable, but revelation 9:107 says otherwise.

> 9:107 And those who build a mosque (the reference is to the mosque built in the neighbourhood of the mosque of Quba', the first mosque built by Muslims) or hurt [the Muslims], to spread unbelief, to disunite [the believers] and to await him (he is said to be Abu 'Amir) who had fought Allah and His Messenger – they will certainly swear that they meant nothing but good. Allah bears witness that they are liars.

> 9:108 Do not stand up there [for prayer]; for a mosque founded on piety from the first day is worthier of you standing in it. Therein are men who love to be purified; and Allah loves those who purify themselves.

What could pass for a parable:

> 9:109 Is one who founds his edifice upon the fear and Good Pleasure of Allah better, or one who founds his edifice upon the brink of a crumbling precipice that will tumble down with him into the Fire of Hell? Allah does not guide the unjust people.

> 9:110 The edifice which they built will continue to be a source of doubt in their hearts, unless their hearts are cut up into pieces. Allah is All-Knowing, Wise.

The Three Sincere Believers Who Lied

No, we are not finished with the controversies surrounding the excursion to Tabuk (see *Allah's Enemies, The Polytheists* for the in-between revelations.) Allah forgave His Messenger for granting all those exemptions along with a group who "almost deviated"; but in the end join the Prophet and went to Tabuk.

> 9:117 Allah has forgiven the Prophet, the Emigrants and the Helpers who followed him in the hour of distress, after the hearts of a group of them had almost deviated. Then He

forgave them; for He is, indeed, Most Kind and Most Merciful towards them.

Back in Medina the Prophet again interviewed those he allowed to stay behind. Those who stuck to their original stories were dismissed with a simple: "May Allah forgive you." When three sincere believers who had accompanied the Prophet on more than one military campaign (two had fought at Badr) admitted to lying, something they now deeply regretted, God's Messenger asked Allah for advice.

As an exemplary punishment from the Prophet, no believers were to talk to the three until Allah had rendered his decision. After forty days, and still no revelation on their score, the Prophet ordered their wives to have nothing to do with them. Ten days later Allah communicated His Decision, which exonerated the three but not before excoriating them, just a little.

> 9:118 And [He also forgave] the three who were left behind till the earth, for all its vastness, became too small for them (meaning they could not find refuge), and their souls were distressed, and they realized there was no refuge from Allah except with Him. Allah then forgave them so that they might repent. Allah is the All-Forgiving, the Merciful.

> 9:119 O you who believe, fear Allah and side with the truthful.

The Prophet returned from Tabuk a more self-confident wary Messenger. His actions on his return secured the home front as he made plans to take his quest for converts and booty further afield.

The Religion of Peace in Persia

"Our aim is not to fight you. Accept Islam the peaceful way, and you will be safe. If not then clear our way to the people so that we may explain this beautiful way of life to them ... if you do not accept any of these conditions then the only alternative is the use of the sword. Before deciding on the third alternative you should keep in mind that I am bringing against you a people who love death more than you love life."

From a letter by Khalid Ibn Al-Walid the leader of the Muslim armies invading Persia to the Persian General Hormuz before the battle of Kadima.

It was a typically bloody conquest with the believers offering no quarter, beheading thousands of surrendered and captured Persian soldiers fulfilling Khalid's pledge to Allah that if He gave them victory "no enemy warrior will be left alive, until their river runs red with blood."

The Muslims may have won the war, but getting the Persian people to accept "the beautiful way of life" may have proven problematic, for Umar, the Caliph at the time of the conquest, to discover another lost verse[39] where Allah included the Zoroastrians as a people of the Book, people who could refuse "the beautiful way of life" and not be put to death, if they agreed to pay the Jizya.

The Magians in revelation 22:17 is the only reference to Zoroastrians in the Koran.

---

[39] It was the same Umar who remembered a verse, which he said must have been lost, where Allah revealed that the punishment for adultery was death by stoning, when the official Koran only stipulates that the guilty parties be lashed 100 times. This claim by Umar, and the Prophet's example, is why women found guilty of intimacy with other than their lawfully-wedded husband are stoned to death to this day (more in *Women and the Koran, Boreal Books, 2012*).

> 22:17 Indeed, the believers, the Jews, the Sabians, the Christians, the Magians and the idolaters – Allah shall decide between them on the Day of Resurrection.

Robert Wright in *The Evolution of God* speculates that verse 22:17 may have been added after the Muslim conquest of Persia to make Islam more palatable to Zoroastrians by including them as a people whom Allah, who "does whatever He pleases", may admit into Paradise.

> By and large the Koran offers no evidence that Muhammad had contact with the Zoroastrians —except for this one verse where they appear out of nowhere and are suddenly eligible for Paradise. It's enough to make you wonder whether this verse wasn't added, or at least amended after Muhammad's death, when the conquest of Persian lands brought many Zoroastrians under Islamic governance.

The Zoroastrians were a people of a book, not the Book, but a book, the *Avesta*; but what about the Sabians?

> There is another reason to suspect that this verse is a product of the post-Muhammad era. It grants salvation not only to Zoroastrians but to "Sabians." To judge by the beliefs of their modern day heirs (sometimes called Mandeans), the Sabians, like the Zoroastrians, would have been hard to fit into the Abrahamic fold; they revered John the Baptist but considered Jesus, Abraham and Moses false prophets. And again (judging by their modern heirs) they would have had another thing in common with Zoroastrians; their residential epicenter was to the east of Muhammad's turf, in modern-day Iraq and Iran, land conquered not by Muhammad but by his successors.
>
> Robert Wright, *The Evolution of God*, p. 394

Who First Destroyed the Birthplace of Zoroaster

Fakhry says Greeks, Moududi says Romans. The "clear revelations" are not always clear even for eminent scholars of the Koran. In Moududi's translation, the Greeks of revelation 30:2 become Romans and those they vanquished are the Iranians who initially vanquished them.

THE GREEKS [or BYZANTINES]

30 Ar-Rum

*In the Name of Allah,
the Compassionate, the Merciful*

30:1 Alif – Lam – Mim.

30:2 The Greeks have been vanquished

30:3 In the nearest part of the land; but after being vanquished, they shall vanquish,

30:4 In a few years. Allah's is the command before and after; and on that day the believers shall rejoice,

30:5 In Allah's support. He supports whom He wills; and He is the Almighty, the Merciful.

30:6 It is Allah's Promise. Allah does not break His Promise, although most people do not know.

The believers rejoiced, according to Moududi, not because of the Byzantine Emperor's victory over the Iranians where he destroyed the birth-place of Zoroaster and ravaged the principal fire-temple of Iran, but the Muslim victory at Badr in 624 over the Meccans which occurred at about the same time.

A Pitch for Martyrs

An imagined pitch for suicide bombers using only verses from one surah.

The *War Surah*, the ninth surah *Repentance*, may be mostly about war but revelations about the conduct of hostilities against the unbelievers are scattered throughout the Koran. These timeless invitations to murder those who do not worship what you worship are often highly concentrated as in the third surah, *The Family of 'Imran*, where the word martyr is first encountered. Like all revelations in the Koran about the need to rid the world of unbelievers, these appeals are addressed to the Prophet's Arab supporters; nonetheless, it is easy to imagine clerics making the same pitch for suicide bombers in Allah's Cause to receptive young men in madrassas and mosques around the world. The target for these recruits will be mainly People of the Book i.e. Jews and Christians, Allah's most hated unbelievers after the polytheists.

Prayers in Islam consist mostly of verses from the Koran, therefore, the pitch I imagined would be to a group of young men gathered for prayer with the prayer leader, the pitchman reciting selected passages from the 3rd surah. A few verses you will find here may have been quoted elsewhere. My comments are in *italics*.

*In the Name of Allah,
the Compassionate, the Merciful*

3:1 Alif, Lam, Mim.

3:2 Allah, there is no God but He, the Living, the Everlasting.

3:3 He has revealed the Book (the Koran) to you in truth, confirming what came before it; and He has revealed the Torah and the Gospel,

3:4 Aforetime, as a guidance to mankind. And He also has revealed the Criterion (the Qur'an *as determiner* of right and wrong). Verily, those who have disbelieved in Allah's Signs, a terrible punishment awaits them; Allah is mighty and stern in retribution.

3:5 Indeed, nothing is hidden from Allah whether on earth or in the heavens.

3:6 It is He Who forms you in the wombs as He pleases; there is no God but he, the Mighty, the Wise.

3:8 Lord, do not cause our hearts to vacillate after You have guided us and grant us Your Mercy. You are indeed the Munificent Giver.

3:10 As to the unbelievers, neither their riches nor their children will avail them anything against Allah; in fact, they shall be the fuel of the Fire.

3:11 Like Pharaoh's people and those before them who denounced Our Revelations. Allah smote them on account of their sins. Allah is Stern in retribution!

3:12 Say to those who disbelieve: "You shall be defeated and driven together into Hell; and what an awful resting place."

The heart of the pitch! Life on earth may be good, but Paradise is better?

3:14 Attractive to mankind is made the love of the pleasures of women, children[40], heaps upon heaps of gold and silver, thoroughbred horses, cattle and cultivatable land. Such is the pleasure of this worldly life, but unto Allah is the fairest return.

3:15 Say: "Shall I tell you about something better than all that?" For those who are God-fearing, from their Lord are gardens beneath which rivers flow, and in which they abide forever [along with] purified spouses and Allah's good pleasure. Allah sees His servants well!

And who are those who seek "purified spouses and Allah's good pleasure"?

3:16 Those who say: "Our Lord, We have believed, so

---

[40] In Yusuf Ali's [1872 – 1953] translation, one of the most widely-known and used in the English-speaking world, children becomes "sons": 3:14 Fair in the eyes of men is the love of things they covet: Women and sons...

forgive us our sins and guard us against the torments of Hell."

3:17 They are the patient, the truthful, the devout, the charitable and the seekers of forgiveness at daybreak (*when battles are usually engaged*).

If you can't believe Allah, who can you believe?

3:18 Allah bears witness that there is no God but He, and so do the angels and men of learning. He upholds justice. There is no God but He, the Mighty and Wise One.

The difference between you and them.

3:19 The [true] religion with Allah is Islam. Those who were given the Book (the Jews and the Christians) did not disagree among themselves, except after certain knowledge came to them, out of envy among themselves. Whoever disbelieves in Allah's Revelations will find Allah Swift in retribution!

Those who are not of your religion must be made to submit to your god, by force if necessary.

3:83 Do they desire a religion other than Allah's, after everyone in the heavens and on earth has submitted to Him willingly or unwillingly; and unto Him they shall all be brought back!

3:85 Whoever seeks a religion other than Islam, it will never be accepted from him, and in the Hereafter he will be one of the losers.

You are the best!

3:110 You were the best nation brought forth to mankind, bidding the right and forbidding the wrong, and believing in Allah. Had the People of the Book believed, it would have been far better for them; some of them are believers, but most of them are sinners.

Not so your enemy!

3:111 They will only cause you a little harm; and if they fight you, they will turn their backs on you (in defeat), and will have no support.

> 3:112 Ignominy shall attend them wherever they are found, unless [they are bound] by a covenant from Allah and a covenant from the people. They will incur Allah's anger, and wretchedness shall be stamped on them, because they disbelieved in Allah's Revelations and killed Prophets unjustly. That is because they disobeyed and exceeded the limits (doing what is unlawful).

Should you harbour doubts about Allah's methods for dealing with the unbelievers i.e. evil-doers.

> 3:128 It is no business of yours whether Allah forgives them or punishes them; for they are indeed evil-doers!

> 3:129 And to Allah belongs what is in the heavens and on earth; He forgives whom He pleases and punishes whom He pleases. Allah is All-Forgiving and Merciful.

> 3:131 And guard yourselves against the Fire which has been prepared for the unbelievers.

Now, obey Allah and the Prophet and ask forgiveness.

> 3:132 And obey Allah and the Messenger, that perchance you may find Mercy.

> 3:133 And hasten to forgiveness from your Lord and a Paradise as wide as the heavens and the earth prepared for the God-Fearing;

A reminder that there is a war on, and that Allah is on their side, therefore, they cannot lose if they are steadfast and don't let their emotions get in the way.

> 3:139 Do not be faint-hearted and do not grieve; you will have the upper hand, if you are true believers.

The first mention of martyrdom!

> 3:140 If you have been afflicted by a wound, a similar wound has afflicted the others (the unbelievers). Such are the times; We alternate them among the people, so that Allah may know who are the believers and choose martyrs from among you. Allah does not like the evildoers!

Will you help Him help the believers and kill the unbelievers?

> 3:141 And that Allah might purify the believers and annihilate the unbelievers.

Don't expect to be first in Paradise if you have not helped Allah rid the world of unbelievers.

> 3:142 Or did you suppose that you will enter Paradise, before Allah has known who were those of you who have struggled, and those who are steadfast.

You were hoping for death to join Him in Paradise, now is your chance.

> 3:143 You were yearning for death before you actually met it. Now you have seen it and you are beholding it.

Role models from the past.

> 3:146 How many Prophets with whom large multitudes have fought; they were not daunted on account of what befell them in the Cause of Allah. They did not weaken or cringe; and Allah loves the steadfast!

> 3:147 Their only words were: "Lord, forgive us our sins and our excess in our affairs. Make firm our feet and grant us victory over the unbelieving people."

> 3:148 Therefore Allah granted them the reward of this life and the excellent reward (Paradise) of the life to come, and Allah loves the beneficent!

Don't trust the unbelievers, trust Me.

> 3:149 O believers, if you obey the unbelievers, they will turn you upon your heels (turning you back from your true religion), and thus you will become complete losers.

> 3:150 Rather, Allah is your Protector, and He is the Best Supporter!

A reminder to keep on killing until victory is assured, and not to be distracted by booty like the believers who fought at the Battle of Uhud, and caused one of the few defeats suffered by the Muslims during the civil war between the pagan Arabs and their Muslim brothers.

> 3:152 Allah fulfilled His Promise to you when, by His Leave, you went on killing them; until you lost heart and

> dissented about the affair and disobeyed, after He had shown you what you cherished (the booty)…

We all have to die sometime.

> 3:168 Those who said to their brethren, while they themselves stayed at home: "Had they obeyed us they would not have been killed?" Say: "Then ward off death from yourselves, if you are truthful."

A gracious forgiving Host will welcome you to Paradise should you die fighting in His Cause.

> 3:157 And were you to be killed or to die in the Way of Allah, forgiveness and Mercy from Allah are far better then what they (the unbelievers) amass.

> 3:158 And were you to die or to be killed, it is unto Allah that you will be gathered.

~~~~~~~~~~~~

Many of the verses quoted here could be considered an incitement to hate and murder. A cleric using these verses, and these verses alone, as part of a recruitment effort for martyrs in a sermon in Arabic (the lingua franca of Islam), in a mosque or madrassa just about anywhere in the Western world, would not be prosecuted because of Western tolerance of hate speech if it is based on revealed truths i.e. scriptures.

Considering the Koran's unrelenting, unmitigated condemnation and de-humanization of unbelievers, this has to be a reason for concern. Ordinary people do not kill other ordinary people unless they have a good reason. Suicide bombers would not do what they do if they were not convinced that their murderess enterprise was sanctioned by Allah. This is why the Koran is such a powerful instrument when it comes to war-mongering.

It is still surprising however, as you read the Koran and are bombarded by Allah's unrelenting hatred of unbelievers (hate-filled-verses which are memorized by children as soon as they can read or mouth the words) and His exhortation to rid the world of them that there are not more young people committing mass murder in His Name. It is even more surprising that more young people are not heeding Allah's and His Messenger's call to arms considering Allah's promised of out-of-this-world hedonistic rewards for those who will expedite the delivery of what He refers to as the "fuel of the Fire."

Yes, the suicide bombers are taking a terrible toll with their indiscriminate mass murder of men, women and children, but the fact that there are not more of them is also proof that humanity's inherent moral core is more resilient to religion's more nefarious influence than some would have us believe, and in that, there is hope.

The Saudi Way

Islam ignited the first and last civil war on the Arabian Peninsula. Having won that war, it embarked on a war of conquest taking Jerusalem only eight years after the surrender of Mecca. Today, followers of the Prophet continue the tradition of seeking to establish Allah's kingdom on earth trough violence, with Wahabism being the driving ideology.

John L. Esposito author of *Unholy War; Terror in the Name of Islam (Oxford University Press)* describes Wahhabism this way:

> Wahhabi theology sees the world in white and black categories — Muslim and non-Muslim, belief and unbelief, the realm of Islam and that of warfare. They regarded all Muslims who [do] not agree with them as unbelievers to be subdued (that is, fought and killed) in the name of Islam.

One of the first to embrace Wahhabi theology was Muhammad Ibn Saud (d. 1765) a local Arab tribal chief. Ibn Saud used the ultra-conservative Wahhabi movement, still according to Esposito, "to legitimate (sic) his jihad to subdue and unite the tribes of Arabia, converting them to this puritanical version of Islam." Ibn Saud still serves as an example for the current rulers of Saudi Arabia who, like their honoured ancestor, look to the teachings of Ibn Abd al-Whahhab for guidance.

Wahhabi theologians have interpreted verse 9:5, *The Verse of the Sword*, as a command from Allah's to wage a non-stop active aggressive campaign to establish His Kingdom on earth. The Ottoman Empire, in 1818 put a stop to Saudi ambitions to spread their fundamentalist version of Islam through violence forcing a change in tactics. The war against the unbelievers can also be fought with your wealth.

> 61:10 O believers, shall I show you a trade which will deliver you from a very painful punishment?
>
> 61:11 Believe in Allah and His Messenger and struggle in

the Cause of Allah with your possessions and yourselves. That is far better for you, if only you knew.

While Saudi Arabia today does not have the military might, Al Qaeda notwithstanding, to spread its puritanical, backward-looking version of Islam by force, it does have the money, and the Koran does say that spending your money .e. possessions to spread Islam gets you a free pass into Paradise – all is forgiven.

> 61:12 He will then forgive your sins and admit you into the Gardens, beneath which rivers flow, and into fine dwellings in the Gardens of Eden. That is the great triumph.

With the discovery of oil and the wealth that came with it, the House that Muhammad Ibn Saud built has been able to spread the Word far and wide by funding Islamic schools on the Wahhabi model, the most notorious being in Pakistan.

Wars Never-Ending

THE SUPPORT

110 An-Nasr

*In the Name of Allah,
the Compassionate, the Merciful*

110:1 When Allah's Support and victory come,

110:2 And you see people entering Allah's religion in throngs;

110:3 Then, magnify the Praise of your Lord and seek His Forgiveness. He is indeed All-Forgiving.

Allah's total proxy victory over the unbelievers, based on revelations about Judgment Day and the conflicts that will rage on its very eve mean that, until then, it is wars never-ending.

War is endemic in Islam, whether it is the never-ending war against unbelievers or believers killing believers in brutal civil wars over leadership and dogma. The Prophet's overwhelming victory over the unbelievers was quickly followed, after his death, by three civil wars under the four so-called Righty Guided Caliphs (Bakr, Umar, Uthman and Ali), the last three assassinated by unhappy believers, heralding an often violent tradition of settling leadership issues, befitting a religion where violence and the threat of violence are pervasive.

Both types of wars, the general war against unbelievers and the bloody pitiless conflicts between believers continue in one form or another to this day, with the second type expected to continue indefinitely, even if Islam is successful in ridding the world of all of those who refuse to submit to the Will of Allah.

AFTERWORD

War and Fantasies

Before the Prophet could attempt to impose Allah's perfect religion on an imperfect world, he first had to convince his fellows Arabs to submit to the Will of Allah and accept him as Allah's anointed spokesperson.

Most would not be swayed to abandon the gods and goddesses of their forefathers and a vicious civil war ensued where the Muslims, except for the rare occasion, would give no quarter.

During this civil war, all the rules of chivalry and fair play that had guided the relationships between the tribes and clans of the Peninsula were abandoned by the Muslims. Only one thing mattered for the believers in this fratricidal war: idol worshippers i.e. pagans had to convert or die!

Convert or die! This simple easy to understand demand from Allah, made known to the believers by His Messenger, the Prophet Muhammad, allowed for a cold-blooded methodical approach to eliminating the Arab opposition, and later non-Arab, and getting converts for Islam.

But even this straightforward strategy might not have worked if Allah and His Messenger had not been able to attract the young men who would be doing the killing and the converting to flock to their banner, as they still do today.

Finding a bride in pre-Islamic and post-Islamic Arabia, if you were not wealthy or powerful was problematic. The fact that rich men could purchase as many women and slave-girls as they could afford, and powerful ones keep as many as they could abscond with, meant that young frustrated fighting men were plentiful.

Allah not only promised these desperate-for-intimacy young men that they could take as slaves or spouses the wives and daughters of the men they killed on His behalf, but should they die in the attempt, He would make it to up to them then and there. They would immediately be admitted into Paradise, no questions asked, and be given a harem more impressive than any found on earth replete with virgins and sexually-adept female-facsimiles i.e. houris all committed to satisfying a young warrior's every sexual fantasies for an eternity.

The surah *Repentance* is mainly about war, one of the reason for the lack of the ubiquitous formula-invocation "in the name of Allah, the Compassionate, the Merciful" which you find at the beginning of every surah but two, the first and the ninth.

The ninth surah can serve as an example on how to carry out a successful campaign against the unbelievers; the key being 1) indoctrinating enough young people into a faith where killing and dying on behalf of a god who murders by proxy is considered doing good for which they will be amply rewarded 2) showing no mercy to anyone no matter their age or gender.

This simple merciless solution to defeating the unbelievers, with terror as a defining component, developed by Allah and His Messenger more than a thousand years ago, and of which the believers are constantly reminded throughout the Koran, is the strategy of Al Qaeda, Islamic State, the Taliban ...

Narrated Abu Huraira:

Allah's Apostle said, "I have been sent with the shortest expressions bearing the widest meanings, and I have been made victorious with terror ... "

Bukhari 52.220

We end *Jihad in the Koran* with the remaining revealed truths from the surah *Repentance* about strategies, tactics, appealing to the baser instincts of those a god needs to slaughter those who will not Submit to His Will on a self-proclaimed spokesperson's say-so, including those who are too young to understand what is being asked of them, most the victim of a vaunted tactic of Allah's Apostle.

When fighting for Allah you are never alone

> 9:16 Did you imagine that Allah would leave you alone before knowing who of you fight [in the Way of Allah] and do not seek supporters besides Allah and His Messenger? Allah is Fully Aware of what you do.

Unbelievers are not welcomed here

> 9:17 The unbelievers should not enter Allah's Mosques bearing witness thereby against themselves that they are

unbelievers. The works of those are vain and in the Fire they will abide forever[41].

9:18 Only he who believes in Allah and the Hereafter, performs the prayers, gives the alms and fears no one but Allah, shall visit Allah's Mosques. Those shall be reckoned among the rightly guided.

Doing wrong by doing right

9:19 Do you consider those, who give the pilgrims water to drink and maintain the Sacred Mosque, like those who believe in Allah and the Hereafter and fight in Allah's Way? They are not alike in Allah's Sight, and Allah will not guide the wrongdoing people.

Stoking the flames of a fratricidal war

9:24 Say: "If your fathers, your sons, your brothers, your spouses, your relatives, the wealth you have gained, a trade you fear might slacken, and dwellings you love are dearer to you than Allah and His Messenger or than fighting in His way, then wait until Allah fulfils His Decree. Allah does not guide the sinful people.

The untouchables

9:28 O believers, the polytheists are truly unclean; so let them not come near the Sacred Mosque after this year of theirs; and if you fear poverty, Allah shall enrich you from His Bounty, if He pleases. Allah is Truly All-Knowing, Wise.

The right religion, the right months and right time to fight

9:36 The number of months, with Allah, is twelve months by Allah's Ordinance from the day He created the heavens and the earth. Four of these are Sacred. This is the right religion, so do not wrong yourselves during them; but fight

---

[41] 22:25 But those who disbelieve and bar others from the Path of Allah and the Sacred Mosque, which We have made open to all people equally – both those who dwell in it and those who visit it. He who wishes in it to incline towards wrongdoing, We shall make him taste a very painful punishment.

An unbeliever caught near the vicinity of the Sacred Mosque must immediately convert or be put to death on the spot. This would suggest that Allah's revelation about the Sacred Mosque being "open to all people equally" applies to believers only.

the polytheists all together just as they fight you all together; and know that Allah is on the side of the righteous.

Another reminder as to who is deserving of Allah's Mercy

9:71 As to the believers, males and females, they are friends of one another. They enjoin what is good and forbid what is evil, perform the prayers, give the alms and obey Allah and His Messenger. It is those on whom Allah will have mercy. Allah is Mighty, Wise.

Another reminder of what is included with that Mercy

9:72 Allah has promised the believers, males and females, Gardens beneath which rivers flow, abiding therein forever, and fair dwellings in the Gardens of Eden. However, Allah's Good Pleasure is greater. That is the great triumph.

Killing and injuring as a good deed

9:120 It is not given to the people of Medina and the desert Arabs around them to stay behind the Messenger of Allah, nor to prefer their own lives to his life for they are afflicted neither by thirst nor fatigue nor hunger in Allah's Way, nor do they take a step that upsets the unbelievers, nor inflict a blow on the enemy but a good deed is recorded for them on account of it. Allah does not allow the beneficent to lose their reward.

9:121 Nor do they spend anything whether small or large, nor cross a valley but it is recorded for them, so that Allah may reward them for the best of their deeds.

Indoctrination and War

9:122 The believers should not all go to war. Why doesn't a company from each group go forth to instruct themselves in religion and admonish their people (those who go to war) when they return, that perchance, they may beware.

Mercy as an attribute of the Prophet.

9:128 There has come to you a Messenger (the Prophet Muhammad) from among yourselves. It grieves him to see you suffer, he cares much for you, and is kind and merciful towards the believers.

Merciful's opposite is merciless

The last revelation of this most ominous of surahs:

> 9:129 But if they turn away, say: "Sufficient for me is Allah; there is no God but He; in Him I put my trust. He is the Lord of the Glorious Throne."

SPECIAL - INDOCTRINATING THE FUTURE

Teach Your Children Well
Children are our future
Teach them well and let them lead the way

Greatest Love of All by Whitney Houston
Lyrics by Michael Masser and Linda Creed

Raising a Holy Warrior

The Prophet's example established fifteen as the age a boy could join the fraternity of holy warriors and participate in the organized slaughter of unbelievers and keep the possessions of those he killed.

Narrated Ibn Umar:

That the Prophet inspected him on the day of Uhud while he was fourteen years old, and the Prophet did not allow him to take part in the battle. He was inspected again by the Prophet on the day of Al-Khandaq (i.e. battle of the Trench) while he was fifteen years old, and the Prophet allowed him to take Part in the battle.

Bukhari 59.423

Narrated Abdur-Rahman bin Auf:

While I was standing in the row on the day (of the battle) of Badr, I looked to my right and my left and saw two young Ansari boys, and I wished I had been stronger than they. One of them called my attention saying, "O Uncle! Do you know Abu Jahl?"

I said, "Yes, What do you want from him, O my nephew?"

He said, "I have been informed that he abuses Allah's Apostle. By Him in Whose Hands my life is, if I should see him, then my body will not leave his body till either of us meet his fate."

I was astonished at that talk. Then the other boy called my attention saying the same as the other had said.

After a while I saw Abu Jahl walking amongst the people. I said (to the boys), "Look! This is the man you asked me about." So, both of them attacked him with their swords and struck him to death and returned to Allah's Apostle to inform him of that.

Allah's Apostle asked, "Which of you has killed him?"

Each of them said, "I Have killed him."

Allah's Apostle asked, "Have you cleaned your swords?"

They said, "No."

He then looked at their swords and said, "No doubt, you both have killed him and the spoils of the deceased will be given to Muadh bin Amr bin Al-Jamuh."

The two boys were Muadh bin 'Afra and Muadh bin Amr bin Al-Jamuh.

Bukhari 53.369

The boys in the preceding hadiths, like your modern teenager or young man revelling in committing atrocities on behalf of Islamic State and Allah, were not born the depraved individuals they have become.

A child is not born a holy warrior. The process of creating suicide bombers and willing executioners for the likes of Islamic State, al-Qaeda, the Taliban, Boko Haram, Al-Shabab ... begins with rote-learning by millions of children around the world of the most pitiless, appalling mainstream piece of religious text ever revealed. One of the most pitiless revelation is also one of the most famous verses of the Koran.

5:38 As for the thieves, whether male or female, cut off their hands in punishment for what they did, as an exemplary punishment from Allah. Allah is Mighty and Wise.

Islamic scholars and religious leaders spend a lot of time trying to explain away pitiless and cruel verses like the above, but, every now and then, the true believers remind them that Allah's unambiguous instructions are not subject to interpretation – a*nd they are correct.* For to do so is to question the wisdom of God; to question God's very sanity thereby destroying the foundation of your beliefs. Before Islamic State, the Taliban, who ruled most of Afghanistan from 1996 until 2001, reminded us about what the Koran is all about.

With the Koran as their legal justification, Taliban gunmen executed women and girls in soccer stadiums. Anonymous, frightened, fragile human beings dressed in oppressive burqas – invisible in life, invisible in death – brought into the stadium in the back of pick-up trucks, forced to kneel on the ground then shot in the back of the head to the obvious pleasure of the bearded young, middle-aged and old men milling around; bearded men displaying the same lack of mercy and compassion that we have come to expect from many of those who utter *In the Name of Allah the Compassionate, the Merciful* every time Allah's name is mentioned.

A Very Special School

If the Taliban, whose very name means *students,* is the product of Islamic schooling, what are such schools teaching children about the meaning of compassion and mercy; not only in Pakistan and the Islamic world but in Western democracies – Canada for instance?

From the web page of an Ottawa Islamic school:

> In the Name of Allah, The Compassionate, The Merciful, Ahlul-Bayt Center is calling on every believer, who heard about the school project, to have a stake in the heavenly awards generated by a work meant to educate Muslim kids about their faith and moral values. May Allah include us all in his mercy and redeem our work by his awards. It is every Muslim's duty to support and preserve the Islamic schools in Ottawa and other cities. The bottom line is that a sincere Islamic education counts in raising Muslim kids based on Quranic teachings and Islamic Moral values.

Are the "Quranic" (sic) teachings and Islamic moral values that this type of school, whether it be in Iran, Pakistan or Canada, claims it will instil in the mind of a child the type of values that you share? Do you believe that these types of values are even deserving of being called "moral values"?

If moral values are defined as being generally accepted standards of good conduct, is what was done to women and girls in Afghanistan what you would consider examples of good conduct? Is what the Koran teaches about mercy and compassion – that some people are not deserving of any for simply not believing in god or the same god you do – morally reprehensible or morally justifiable?

Do you consider it morally acceptable that women and girls can be sexually assaulted as long as it is done in a marriage setting? Do you consider it morally acceptable that a wife can be beaten by her husband if he fears she is going to sin or has sinned? Do you consider it morally acceptable that males are taught that females are their inferior and females are instructed to accept this lesser status because the God of the Koran says that is the way it must be?

These are important questions. Your future, the future of your children may depend on your response to the real moral and ethical dilemma raised by these questions.

What about the Koran's relentless graphic description of sadistic torture and pain? As an adult you may be able to dismiss Allah's bragging about torturing and burning men, women and children, in His Hell as metaphorical excesses, sadistic flights of fancy, but what about Muslim children? Children raised in the Islamic faith are encouraged, if not compelled, at the earliest age to memorize the Koran; the prize for the best memorizer being a choice place in heaven.

There is a very common ceremony practiced throughout most of the Muslim world called Khatmi-Qur'an. It is the ceremony to recognize and celebrate a child's first full reading of the Koranic text in Arabic. Muslim children in traditional Islamic societies or families are expected to have read and more or less understood the Koran, in Arabic, from cover to cover before they reach the age of seven.

What kind of twisted perception of the concept of mercy and compassion will such children be left with after memorizing the following verses about Allah, on Judgement Day, not caring about the people that He condemns to burn in Hell in perpetuity for not believing in Him, "for what you used to do?"

> 52:13 On the Day they will be driven into the Fire of Hell by force.

> 52:14 "This is the Fire which you used to deny.

> 52:15 "Is this magic or do you not see?

> 52:16 "Burn in it. Bear up or do not bear up; it is the same for you. You are only rewarded for what you used to do."

What kind of warped understanding of the concept of mercy and compassion will Muslim children be left with after reading about how the *Compassionate One* takes obvious pleasure in the punishment He inflicts.

> 11:105 The day (*Judgement Day*) it comes, no soul shall speak without His Leave. Some of them shall be wretched, some happy.
>
> 11:106 As for the wretched, they shall be in the Fire; they shall have therein groaning and moaning;

Lessons in Cruelty

What happens to the mind, to the personality of a child who commits, must commit to memory, not only the hate filled verses we have discussed so far, but others that are even more impressive in their attention to detail when it comes to the deliberate, cold-blooded application of torture. For instance, the *Compassionate One* replacing the burnt skin of unbelievers burning in His Hell so that the torment of their skin roasting in His Fire never ends.

> 4:56 Those who have disbelieved Our Signs, We shall surely cast them into the Fire; every time their skins are burnt, We will replace them by other skins, so that they might taste the punishment. Allah indeed is Mighty and Wise!

In Allah's Hell, the fantastical vision of pain and torment quickly gives way to the more mundane, but just as gruesome, just as painful torture and never-ending suffering with which any child can relate. For a non-believing adult the following brutality may seem like the plot of some of the more violent Saturday morning cartoons their kids watch. For believing children the following is real, and not the product of a cartoonist's imagination. Somewhere in time and space, in Allah's bizarre universe, He is actually doing to real people what some children may fantasize about but eventually dismiss, as they grow older, as *immoral, sadistic behaviour*.

> 14:16 Behind him is Hell, and he is given stinking water to drink.
>
> 14:17 He sips it but can hardly swallow it, and death surrounds him from every side, but he will not die; and beyond this is still a terrible punishment.
>
> ----
>
> 18:29 And say: "The Truth is from your Lord. Whoever wishes, let him believe; and whoever wishes, let him disbelieve." We have prepared for the wrongdoers a Fire

whose canopy encompasses them all. If they call for relief, they will be relieved with water like molten brass which scalds the faces. Wretched is that drink and wretched is the resting-place!

22:19 Here are two adversaries who dispute about their Lord. To the unbelievers, garments of fire shall be cut up and over their heads boiling water shall be poured;

22:20 Whereby whatever is in their bellies and in their skin shall be melted.

22:21 And for them are iron rods (to beat their heads with).

22:22 Every time they want, in their gloom, to get out of it (the Fire), they are brought back into it. [And it is said to them]: "Taste the agony of burning."

Such is the punishment from Allah for not believing in His Book and His Messenger, and don't bother saying you're sorry, it won't do you any good.

23:101 And when the Trumpet is blown, they will have no kinship to bind them on that Day and they will not question one another.

23:102 Then, those whose scales are heavy – those are the prosperous.

23:103 But those whose scales are light – those are the ones who have lost their souls. In Hell they will dwell forever.

23:104 The Fire lashes their faces, and therein they shrivel.

23:105 "Were not My Signs (this Qur'an) recited to you, but you used to denounced them as lies?"

23:106 They will say: "Lord, our misery overcame us and we were are an erring people.

23:107 "Lord, bring us out of it (Hell); then, if we revert we are indeed wrongdoers."

23:108 He (Allah) said: "Rot in it and do not talk to Me.

It's all about winners and losers, with the losers getting all the pain and the winners all the pleasure.

> 23:109 "There was a group of My servants who used to say: 'Lord, we believe, so forgive us and have mercy on us; you are the best of the merciful.'
>
> 23:110 "But you took them for a laughingstock, till they made you forget My Name, while you were mocking them.
>
> 23:111 "I have rewarded them this day for their forbearance, making them the winners."

Pleasure or pain, which will it be?

> 47:15 The likeness of the Garden which the God-fearing have been promised is this: rivers of water not stagnant, rivers of milk whose taste has not changed, rivers of wine delighting its drinkers and rivers of distilled honey. Therein they have every variety of fruit and forgiveness from their Lord too. Are they to be compared with those who dwell in the Fire forever and are given to drink boiling water which will rip up their bowels?

What happens to the mind of a child who commits to memory, not only the horrific descriptions of what Allah will do in His Hereafter to those who refused to submit to His Will, but what He expects the believers to do, in the here-and-now, to those who would abandon Islam. On at least three occasions, Allah, in the person of Pharaoh, will remind the child labouring to memorize verses of inconceivable brutality that Allah's recommended punishment for leaving Islam is having your hands and feet cut off on alternate sides then to be crucified upon the trunks of trees – palm trees if they can be found.

As the child memorises these techniques for inflicting unbelievable pain and humiliation on those who would dare leave Allah's perfect religion for one less perfect or for no religion at all, he will be reminded that childhood offers no protection from a vengeful, unforgiving god when it comes to unbelievers and apostates. The spontaneous, cold-blooded murder of a child by Khidr because Allah fears his lack of commitment to Islam will cause his parents distress, forever etched in the young impressionable mind: *this God does not flinch at killing children who don't do as they are told and replacing them with children who will.*

> 18:74 Then they departed; but when they met a boy, <u>he (Khidr) killed him</u>. Moses said: "Have you killed an

innocent person who has not killed another? You have surely committed a horrible deed."

18:80 "As for the boy, his parents were believers; so we feared that he might overwhelm them with oppression and unbelief.

18:81 "So we wanted that their Lord might replace him with someone better in purity and closer to mercy.

What happens to the mind of a child who commits these horrifying descriptions of pain and suffering to memory? What happens to the mind of a child who is required to repeat many of these cruel, pitiless, sadistic verses as part of the five daily mandatory prayers[42] to a god who claims to be the personification, the embodiment of compassion and mercy?

THE BACKBITER
104 Al-Humazah

*In the Name of Allah,
the Compassionate, the Merciful*

104:1 Woe unto every backbiter and slanderer,

104:2 Who amasses wealth and counts it diligently.

104:3 He thinks that his wealth will make him immortal.

104:4 Not at all; he shall be cast into the Smasher.

104:5 And if only you knew what is the Smasher.

104:6 It is Allah's kindled Fire,

104:7 Which attains even the hearts.

104:8 Upon them it is closing in;

104:9 On pillars stretch out.

What do Muslim children dream about after reading about the *Smasher* and people bound to pillars while the *Smasher* creeps towards their hearts to burn it?

What do they fantasise about during their waking hours? Do

---

[42] All five mandatory ritual prayers must begin with the first chapter of the Koran followed by a minimum of three verses from the Koran.

they ever forget the tortured and tormented verses, including those that encourage mutilation of alleged wrongdoers, which they memorized under the benevolent encouragement of their teachers, imams, parents and guardians?

What do these well-intentioned teachers of Islamic "morality" think they are doing? What do they think they are doing when they tell the children to pay particular attention to revelations about Allah's heroes such as the many Prophets who disowned parents, family members and close relatives who refused to submit to His Will?

What do they think they are doing when they invite children to read Allah's often repeated instructions not to associate with unbelievers, and the even more compelling revelations that demand that Christians and Jews who are invited to become Muslim but decline, and refuse to pay a ransom to save their lives, be murdered in cold-blood?

What do they think they are doing when they invite children to read revelations that damn and curse people who believe in more than one god, Indians for example, and instruct the believers to kill them on the spot if they are invited to become Muslim but refuse; that for polytheists not even a ransom can save their lives?

Lebensraum

Are Islamic schools and mosques raising another generation of *willing executioners* unable to empathise with the people, the unbelievers, for whom Allah shows no mercy and reserves such a gruesome, painful agonizing fate?

Are the Saudis, perhaps unwittingly, taking a page out of Mein Kampf by funding madrassas on the Wahabi extremist model around the world; madrassas which teach children that Islam is the master religion and all that this implies, including murder on a genocidal scale[43]? Hitler, in Mein Kampf, looked to the East for what he called

---

[43] Based on Muslim chronicles of the period, and the demographic calculations done by historian K.S. Lal in his book Growth of Muslim Population in Medieval India, the largest known slaughter of followers of a lesser god, or gods, occurred during the Muslim conquest of large parts of the Indian subcontinent e.g. modern-day Pakistan and Bangladesh.

Dr. Lal estimates that between 1000 CE and 1500 CE the population of Hindus decreased by 80 million; meaning that for much of that period the death rate among Hindus exceeded their birthrate. If the eminent historian's estimates are even

Lebensraum, literally "living space" for the master race. This living space was to be acquired through extermination, enslavement and sterilization of non-Arian races. It was the moral duty of every NAZI to ensure the survival of the master race by whatever means at his or her disposal.

Allah gives tacit approval to the followers of what is understood to be the superior religion (revelations 3:85, 48:28) – and who He has made successors to an overcrowded planet (revelation 35:39) – to deprive those who belong to inferior religions, or no religion at all, of their possessions and their lives.

> 3:85 Whoever seeks a religion other than Islam, it will never be accepted from him, and in the Hereafter he will be one of the losers.

> 48:28 It is He Who sent forth His Messenger with the guidance and the religion of truth, that He may exalt it above every other religion. Allah suffices as Witness.

> 35:39 It is He Who made you successors in the lands. Then he who disbelieves, his unbelief will recoil upon him; and their unbelief will only increase the unbelievers in contempt in the sight of their Lord. No, their unbelief will only increase the unbelievers in perdition.

Will this piece of entitlement dogma lead to even greater atrocities then when it was the alleged superior race which laid claim to exclusivity of lebensraum?

Will the practitioners of the master religion, one day, with the authority granted them by the Koran, see it as their religious and moral duty to cull an overpopulated starving planet to ensure not only the survival, but the supremacy of the master religion and those who believe, until their god can bring an end to His Creation?

Willing Executioners

In his book *Hitler's Willing Executioners: Ordinary Germans and the Holocaust*, Daniel Jonah Goldhagen presents evidence that the demonizing of the Jews by the Christian churches for the alleged

---

remotely accurate, this period would have witnessed the largest cold-blooded killing of an indigenous people in all written history.

murder of Christ and other offences pre-disposed Germans to accept and participate in the murder of millions of Jews. What kind of monsters is the Koran giving birth to by its relentless, unremitting insistence that unbelievers are creatures not deserving of any mercy or compassion. That unbelievers are only deserving of the most horrible punishment?

Most parents try to protect their children from the make-believe violence on television, reminding them that it is all make-believe, and that this is not how normal, civilized people behave. In madrassas, teachers are not expected to tell the children who are memorizing the Koran under their supervision and with their assistance that the violence is not real or that extreme, pitiless cruelty or any kind of brutality is not acceptable when dealing with those who won't submit to the will of Allah. Perhaps it is time for the West to heed the advice of a woman who knows. Ayaan Hirsi Ali would restrict religious teachings to places of worship and the home so that children can get a respite from the relentless bombardment of the word of God and learn to appreciate the values inherent in a secular society free from religion's more nefarious influence.[44]

If nothing is done to curb this schooling in hate and sadism, what truly horrifying events are we setting in motion as the world gives rise to the next generation of Hitler-like leadership, similar to the one we find in Iran, where burning the unbelievers in an atomic fire is seen as doing God's work on earth? Only doing what Allah would do if he were here – gather the "kindling for His Hell", the "fuel for His Fire."

I realize I may be placing too much emphasis on one preponderant aspect of the Koran, the sadism and the horrific cruelty, but that is in large part what the Koran is all about. Muslims and non-Muslims should be concerned with the impact of reading, of memorizing such violent, pitiless text on young minds.

---

[44] Madrassas may also be contributing to the feeling of alienation among Muslim youths in countries that have national standards for education and which test for proficiency in a wide variety of subjects. The emphasis on memorizing the Koran and on learning Arabic in traditional madrassas means that madrassa students tend to do poorly on these tests. An example is Thailand where, according to Jeffrey Simpson writing in the Globe and Mail "The average Muslim student spends more time in school than the Buddhist [but] do appreciably worse on national educational tests..." *Battle of the minds' is dividing Thailand's identity* March 3, 2007

Remembering Nicholas Berg

What children raised on hate and mercilessness become capable of! The Ottawa Citizen's description of the execution of Nicholas Berg by Abu Musab al-Zarqawi (al-Qaeda's top man in Iraq, at the time) on May 7, 2004:

> Zarqawi literally hacked and sawed with his knife the neck of the young twenty-six year-old idealist from Pennsylvania while he screamed in agony. In the words of Dan Garner writing in the Ottawa Citizen, Zarqawi "sawed back and forth as if he were cutting a thick rope. Berg screamed and screamed and screamed. Zarqawi kept sawing back and forth, back and forth, cutting on this side, cutting on that. Finally, Nicholas Berg's head left his body. Zarqawi clutched it by the hair and raised it to the camera as he and his men shouted Allahu Akbar! God is Great, God is Great."

www.ingramcontent.com/pod-product-compliance
Lightning Source LLC
Chambersburg PA
CBHW051754040426
42446CB00007B/362